LEGENDS OF WARFARE
UNITS

US Marine Corps in Vietnam

Vehicles, Weapons, and Equipment

DAVID DOYLE

SCHIFFER MILITARY

4880 Lower Valley Road   Atglen, PA 19310

Edited by Bob Biondi
Designed by Justin Watkinson
Type set in Impact/Minion Pro/Univers LT Std

ISBN: 978-0-7643-6260-6
Printed in China

Published by Schiffer Publishing, Ltd.
4880 Lower Valley Road
Atglen, PA 19310
Phone: (610) 593-1777; Fax: (610) 593-2002
E-mail: Info@schifferbooks.com
www.schifferbooks.com

For our complete selection of fine books on this and related subjects, please visit our website at www.schifferbooks.com.
You may also write for a free catalog.

Schiffer Publishing's titles are available at special discounts for bulk purchases for sales promotions or premiums. Special editions, including personalized covers, corporate imprints, and excerpts, can be created in large quantities for special needs. For more information, contact the publisher.

We are always looking for people to write books on new and related subjects. If you have an idea for a book, please contact us at proposals@schifferbooks.com.

Acknowledgments

This book would not have been possible without the gracious help of many individuals and institutions, in particular the combat photographers who captured the images reproduced on these pages. Further, I am indebted to the staffs of the National Archives and the USMC Gray Research Center, as well as Dana Bell, the late David E. Harper, and Pat Stansell. Their generous and skillful assistance adds immensely to the quality of this volume. In addition, the Lord has blessed me with a wonderful wife, Denise, who has tirelessly scanned thousands of photos and documents for this and numerous other books. Beyond that, she is an ongoing source of support and inspiration.

All photos are from the National Archives and Records Administration unless otherwise noted.

Contents

Foreword

In this book, like countless others, it is inevitable that names like Lyndon Johnson, Robert Strange McNamara, and William C. Westmoreland will appear. It is unfortunate, because while these men and others like them influenced the Vietnam War, they did not fight the Vietnam War. The fighting and the hardships of the US experience in Vietnam were borne on the broad shoulders of "average" Americans; some professional military, some volunteers, and some drafted. Some with college educations, others with only a grade school education, family men (and women), others confirmed bachelors. It is those largely unnamed masses who donned the uniforms of the US armed services—Navy, Air Force, Army, Coast Guard—or as celebrated in this volume, the United States Marines, and truly fought the war. Whether on patrol, in a foxhole, or in a supply dump, these men paid for the decisions made by the men whose names are familiar, either in time away from loved ones or watching loved ones, their brothers in arms, die or be maimed, or being killed themselves.

This volume is a photographic summary of the US Marines' time on the ground in Vietnam. For this reason, wherever possible, the Marines in the photographs have been identified. Some may not be general officers, or Medal of Honor winners, but they are important. They did their job. They are sons, brothers, husbands, fathers—immeasurably important to someone—and immeasurably important to our nation, deserving of respect, and, wherever possible, being called by name.

Unfortunately, in many cases the combat photographer did not record the name—this is not a criticism—and frankly, I am impressed that in the heat of combat these men could compose and take excellent photos. Those Marines, in the official captions, are referred to as "a Marine," or if with their brothers, "Marines."

This too is fitting in a way. Near our nation's capital, on a low hill, as I write this, and as you read this months or years later, an immaculate sentinel of the 3rd US Army Infantry Regiment is solemnly standing watch over the tombs of three US servicemen, "known but to God," from unknown branches of service, from three wars (the Vietnam tomb is empty, the former occupant having been identified as Air Force lieutenant Michael J. Blassie). Their vigil, one of the most solemn in the nation, renders honor to those unknown men, and through them, all US servicemen who sacrificed in those wars.

Likewise, when you gaze upon the faces of the unidentified Marines in this book, let them in a similar manner represent to you ALL the Marines who served in Vietnam.

Introduction

As I write this, over forty-five years have passed since MSgt. Juan Valdez, commanding the Marine Security Guard at the Saigon Embassy, climbed aboard the last helicopter leaving the embassy, bringing with him the US flag. However, the topic of the US involvement in Vietnam remains a polarizing issue. Largely gone are the criticisms of the individual troops who served the nation, but remaining are some who still argue the "why" of the troops, or the "how" of the way the war was conducted. Lingering still is considerable bitterness, with veterans stung by their treatment and, in some cases, haunted by their experiences in Southeast Asia.

Situated on the Indochinese Peninsula, Vietnam borders China to the north and Laos and Cambodia to the west, while the Gulf of Thailand and the South China Sea form its remaining boundaries.

The French colonized the area, and by 1887 the region was known as French Indochina. The French introduced a great deal of Western culture into the area, and missionaries, chiefly Catholic, expanded Christianity throughout the region, despite the massacre of 40,000 Vietnamese Christians by members of the Cần Vương movement during this time.

The French remained in control of the area until the Japanese invaded in 1940. For a time the Vichy French remained in puppet government and allowed 140,000 Japanese troops to be stationed in the nation, until March 1945, when the Japanese took over. Late 1944 and early 1945 was also the time of the Vietnamese Famine, which brought with it deaths that some estimates place at two million people, and also set the stage for the rise of Communism.

The Việt Minh, which had begun to emerge as a force in 1941, seized the famine as a cause to rally around, an effort that gained momentum following Japan's defeat in 1945. In 1946, the Việt Minh began a guerrilla war against the French, who were reestablishing control in French Indochina. This war continued until July 1954, shortly after the fall of the besieged French forces at Điện Biên Phủ, a battled that concluded with the capture of 11,721 French troops. The Eisenhower administration considered sending US Marines to assist the French during the siege, but ultimately rejected the concept.

The Geneva Accords of 1954 dissolved French Indochina and divided Vietnam into North and South Administrative Zones, with a broad Demilitarized Zone (DMZ) between them, roughly along the seventeenth parallel. While it was intended that the country would be reunited by elections in July 1956, the accord provided a 300-day free movement period during which Vietnamese could relocate to their preference of the northern or southern region. During this time almost a million Vietnamese, primarily Christians, moved from the north to the south. This relocation was aided by the French navy and air force, as well as the US Navy and Marine Corps. The US effort was dubbed Operation Passage to Freedom.

During the 1956 elections, fraudulent balloting led to Ngô Đình Diệm being recognized as the head of state. Ironically, most experts and analysts believe that Diệm would have handily won a legitimate election. Three days after the October 23, 1955, voting, Diệm proclaimed himself president of the new Republic of Vietnam, but the fraud would undermine his control. This was further exacerbated by what many, including the US government, saw as Diệm's persecution of Buddhists. This led to a late 1963 coup by the military and non-Communist Vietnamese nationalists. The US reportedly knew in advance of the planned coup and agreed to do nothing to intervene. The coup culminated in Diệm's assassination on November 2, 1963, inside the rear of an M113 armored personnel carrier. In the view of many, this coup is what directly led to the extensive US troop involvement in Vietnam.

The Communist leader Hồ Chí Minh, upon learning of the assassination, reportedly stated: "I can scarcely believe the Americans would be so stupid."

The Political Bureau of the Central Committee Communist Party of Vietnam was even more direct, releasing a statement saying, "The consequences of the November 1 coup d'état will be contrary to the calculations of the US imperialists. . . . Diệm was one of the strongest individuals resisting the people and Communism. Everything that could be done in an attempt to crush the revolution was carried out by Diệm. Diệm was one of the most competent lackeys of the US imperialists."

In the aftermath, several military governments claimed power before, ultimately, Air Marshal Nguyễn Cao Kỳ and General Nguyễn Văn Thiệu took control in mid-1965.

North Vietnamese subversives had begun working to topple the South Vietnamese government immediately and were soon joined by the South Vietnam–based Việt Cộng, which themselves were controlled by the Military Commission of the Party Central Committee in Hanoi. In November 1961, US president John F. Kennedy decided to increase aid to the Diệm government. The number of US military advisors in Vietnam, who had first arrived in 1950 and in 1960 had numbered 685, increased to 12,000 by 1962. Included in those 12,000 were eighteen USMC advisors and a Marine helicopter squadron and support elements, code-named SHUFLY.

The August 2, 1964, battle between three North Vietnamese navy torpedo boats and the destroyer DD-731, the USS *Maddox*, 28 miles off North Vietnam in international waters and supported by F-8 Crusaders flying from CVA-14 USS *Ticonderoga*, would change things dramatically. This event led to the US Congress passing the Gulf of Tonkin Resolution, named for the body of water in which the battle occurred, on August 7, 1964. This joint resolution of Congress authorized the president of the United States (at that time, Johnson), without a formal declaration of war, to use conventional military force to assist "any member or protocol state of the Southeast Asia Collective Defense Treaty," which included South Vietnam.

Although during his 1964 election campaign, Johnson had said, "We are not about to send American boys 9 or 10,000 miles away from home to do what Asian boys ought to be doing for themselves," the passage of the Gulf of Tonkin Resolution allowed him to reverse course.

CHAPTER 1
The Marines Have Landed: 1965

On February 7, 1965, the Việt Cộng (VC) attacked Camp Holloway near Pleiku. Constructed by the US Army 81st Transportation Company in August 1962, Camp Holloway served to support helicopter operations of the South Vietnam and Free World Military Forces in the Central Highlands. The VC attack killed nine Americans, wounded an additional 126, and destroyed ten aircraft. Later that day, President Johnson announced the withdrawal of all US dependents from Vietnam. In addition, he stated, "I have ordered the deployment to South Vietnam of a HAWK air defense battalion." That battalion was Battery A, USMC 1st Light Anti-Aircraft Missile Battalion (LAAM), and it was sent from Okinawa to Da Nang. The move would require fifty-two C-130 flights, moving 315 tons of equipment and 309 Marines. Nine days later, the rest of the battalion, with the exception of Battery C, which remained on Okinawa, arrived in Da Nang by ship.

On February 21, 1964, in yet another coup, the commander in chief of the Vietnamese armed forces was changed. The continuing civil unrest alarmed the commander of the Military Assistant Command, Vietnam (MACV), Gen. William C. Westmoreland. Westmoreland was concerned that the South Vietnamese army would be unable or unwilling to protect the US forces on the ground, especially at Da Nang. His deputy, Lt. Gen. John Throckmorton, advocated a three-battalion Marine expeditionary brigade be deployed to secure the air base. Westmoreland, hoping to limit the number of Americans in Vietnam, preferred to send two battalions instead, and this was communicated to President Johnson.

The first US ground troops committed in force to the war in Vietnam were 3,500 men of the 3rd Battalion Landing Team, 9th Marine Expeditionary Brigade, who, with the approval of the government of Vietnam, landed on Red Beach 2 near Da Nang on the afternoon of March 8, 1965. Flying in from Okinawa that afternoon aboard C-130s would be the 1st Battalion, 3rd Marines. These Marines were soon supplemented by the 2nd Battalion, 9th Marines, on July 4, 1965. The arrival of those two units began what would become the longest war in USMC history, and by the end of 1965 the number of Marines in Vietnam had soared to 38,000.

Other than heavy seas, the landing at Red Beach was uneventful, and the Marines were greeted by university students with flowers. Highway 1 was closed to all but military traffic, and at 9:45 the Marines began to convoy to the air base, with the streets often lined with waving, cheering Vietnamese.

The Marines were there to protect American personnel and interests, and the landing order issued by the Joint Chiefs of Staff on March 7 specified that "the US Marine Force will not, repeat will not, engage in day-to-day actions against the Viet Cong." The Da Nang Air Base was the primary installation to be protected, but beyond that, General Westmoreland stated, "Overall responsibility for the defense of Da Nang area remains a RVNAF [Republic of Vietnam Armed Forces] responsibility."

Six days after arriving in Vietnam, LCpl. Robert John Achas of Springfield, Illinois, of the 1st Platoon, India Company, 3rd Battalion, 9th Marine Regiment, 3rd Marine Division, was killed at Hill 327 on March 14, 1965, becoming the first USMC casualty of the war. Adding to the tragedy, Achas was killed and two other Marines were wounded by so-called "friendly fire" while returning from patrol.

On March 31, aviators of Marine Air Group 16 were tasked with providing helicopter support for ARVN Operation Quyet Thang 512, and during the course of this operation, two Marines were killed and seventeen were wounded, and a Marine UH-34D was shot down.

Further examination of the US effort in Vietnam led to the decision to send two more battalions of Marines in 1965. One of these battalions would join the first two at Da Nang, while the fourth would be stationed at the Hue / Phu Bai airstrip, 8 miles south of Hue, where they would be responsible for protecting the US Army 8th Radio Research Unit as well as the nearby small airfield. Westmoreland had visions of moving helicopter operations from Da Nang to the Phu Bai airstrip to relieve congestion at Da Nang.

This plan was not universally endorsed, with the Marines' Lt. Gen. Victor H. Krulak, commanding general of Fleet Marine Force, Pacific (FMFPac), writing, "Here is an example of where dollar economics wagged the tail of the military deployment. Phu Bai is as tactically indefensible as anyone could imagine. General Westmoreland was determined, however, that we should go there because of the existence of the 8th RRU. There was an investment of probably five million dollars in the unit. It was firmly locked to the Phu Bai plain[,] and he was determined not to see it move. He was reinforced by the testimony of experts who said its location was particularly good from a "technical" point of view. Whether or not this is true and our own . . . people strongly questioned it, he insisted that we go there despite the tremendous land barrier between Da Nang and Phu Bai, difficulty of providing logistical support, and the many better uses to which a Marine BLT could have been put. I believe we would have been better off by far to have moved the 8th RRU to another place and to have kept our forces more concentrated."

On April 1, in addition to approving an increase of US troops in Vietnam, President Johnson made a decision that would have far-reaching impact on the Marines in Vietnam, changing their mission such that they could be used "in active combat under conditions to be established and approved by the Secretary of Defense in consultation with the Secretary of State."

Entering Vietnam from Okinawa and Japan were Regimental Landing Team (RLT) 3, under the command of Col. Edwin B. Wheeler. This unit was composed of RLT headquarters and BLT 2/3, commanded by Lt. Col. David A. Clement, and BLT 3/4, drawn from the newly arrived 4th Marines.

In addition, air elements in the form of Marine Air Support Squadron (MASS) 2 and VMFA-531 were deployed. The latter was the result of Gen. Westmoreland requesting an F-4 Phantom unit, since the type could perform strike missions in the north as well as tactical missions in the south.

The use of Marine ground forces, and their area of responsibility, was subject to a considerable amount of political negotiation with the Vietnamese. For example, in the area of the Phu Bai airfield, it was decided that the villages bordering the base to the north and east would be defended by the Vietnamese, while the 3rd Battalion, 4th Marines Tactical Area of Responsibility (TAOR) would defend the installation itself, and the areas to the south and west, "with emphasis on quick reaction offensive moves."

On April 20, the Marines at Da Nang and Phu Bai began patrols outside their TAORs but were accompanied by ARVN soldiers and Vietnamese civil affairs officers to placate the area villagers. Two days later, the Marines on patrol had their first firefight after encountering about 105 Việt Cộng near Binh Thai,

9 miles southwest of Da Nang. During this battle, one Marine was wounded and one Việt Cộng killed. A second encounter two days later resulted in two dead Việt Cộng at the cost of two Marines.

While Marines were patrolling, and bleeding, in the brush of Vietnam, Secretary of Defense Robert McNamara was meeting in Honolulu with Generals Westmoreland and Wheeler, Adm. Sharp, and others concerning the US presence in Vietnam. The conclusion that was reached involved introducing a further 42,000 US troops into the country, including 5,000 more Marines. The Marines, including three reinforced battalions and three jet aircraft squadrons, were to be based at the coastal inlet of Chu Lai, 57 miles southeast of Da Nang, to which it was connected by the paved Highway 1. This tactic was approved by President Johnson on April 25, furthering an increase in Marines in Vietnam begun earlier in the year, which would continue to increase. By June, there were 18,100 Marines in Vietnam, a number that would more than double to 38,200 by December and reach 56,500 by September 1966.

The Marines in Vietnam, under Lt. Gen. Lewis W. "Lew" Walt, strove to make allies of Vietnamese villagers. Walt, who was fond of pointing out that 130,000 Vietnamese lived within mortar range of the Da Nang airfield, recognized that the key to the success of the mission was to ensure that more Vietnamese subscribed to US ideology than subscribed to Communist ideology.

Walt instituted what became known as the Combined Action Program (CAP). In this program, Marine rifle squads were paired with South Vietnamese militia platoons, forming a combined action company. These Marines lived and worked 24/7 with their Vietnamese counterparts.

When President Johnson halted bombing after Christmas 1965, US reconnaissance showed that the North Vietnamese were moving troops and supplies across the demilitarized zone (DMZ). About 14 miles south of the DMZ, along the route of Highway 9, which connected the Mekong River valley with the coastal plain, was Khe Sanh. Home of a US Army Green Beret camp, Khe Sanh was also the base of the covert US Air Force unit "Tiger Hound," which pioneered forward air-controller functions. Beginning in the fall of 1966, there would be Marines posted at Khe Sanh, and a year later a multiple-battalion effort fought for and won the hilltop positions around Khe Sanh, which then became Marine Corps strongholds. One of these, Con Thien, would become the scene of the longest continuous battle of the Marines in Vietnam. From May through September, the North Vietnamese assaulted and besieged this position. Holding the position involved several Marine battalions as well as ARVN forces.

Landing craft LCU-1476 from the USS *Vancouver* (LPD-2) approaches Red Beach 2 to disgorge its load of Marine M48A3s on March 8, 1965. These men and other elements of the 9th Marine Expeditionary Brigade were part of the USMC force sent to secure the Da Nang airport and its surrounding area, which was the first major deployment of the USMC in the Vietnamese conflict.

A Marine M37 Dodge of Battalion Landing Team 3/9 passes under a lavishly made banner at the entrance to the city of Da Nang, welcoming the US Marine Corps on March 8, 1965. BLT-3/9 landed to become a part of the 9th MEB from ships across Red Beach 2, since BLT-1/3 landed by air at Da Nang airfield.

A Marine UH-34D sets down on Hill 327 amid a cloud of dust blown up by its rotor blades on March 10, 1965. An M274 Mechanical Mule (*in the foreground*) waits for the incoming supplies. Hill 327, an important terrain feature, sat just west of Da Nang and was the highest point in the 9th MEB area of operations. Occupying it was an immediate objective.

Marines of K Company, Battalion Landing Team 3/9, operate an M40 106 mm recoilless rifle in a prepared position on Hill 327, also on March 10. Although originally designed as an antitank weapon, the breech-loading, single-shot M40 was an integral part of the USMC small-unit fire support in the 1950s and 1960s.

A bulldozer gives a hand to an M422 Mighty Mite quarter-ton tactical truck on the afternoon of April 10, 1965, as troops and equipment leave the Red Beach area where portions of the 2nd Battalion, 3rd Marines, landed. This landing was the second phase of the initial USMC buildup in the Da Nang area.

Another M422 advances at the head of a line of vehicles toward the city of Da Nang on April 12, 1965. Curious Vietnamese watch. Behind the M422 are two M38A1s, and at least two of the vehicles are equipped with deep-wading snorkels. Mid-America Research Corp. designed the M422 specifically for the Marine Corps in the early 1950s, but American Motors manufactured it. The M422 appears to be marked as a member of the HQ Company of the 12th Regiment (Artillery).

Marines of BLT 3/4 rush out of the doors of their LVTP-5A1 landing vehicles on the morning of April 14, 1965. The LVTP-5 (Landing Vehicle, Tracked, Personnel) was the Marine Corps' primary amphibious armored fighting vehicle. Manufactured by Borg-Warner, its design was based on improving the successful wartime LVT series of vehicles—albeit with a much-higher load capacity. The vehicles could safely transport up to thirty-four fully equipped Marines.

After their landing at Red 2 in the morning of on April 14, 1965, the Marines of Battalion Landing Team 3/4 were lifted by helicopter to Phu Bai to relieve elements of the 2nd Battalion, 3rd Marines. Here, they wait for the word to move out to their new positions while the 2/3 prepares to embark in the same helicopter for the return trip to Da Nang.

The remaining elements of BLT 3/4 stayed on board their transports with the Navy Task Group, then moving north to the mouth of the Hue River. There, the Marines and their equipment would unload into landing craft for the trip to Hue City and then make the 14-kilometer trip to Phu Bai by road. Here, an M35A1 2.5-ton truck with trailer in tow is en route from Hue on April 14.

In the scrub some distance from the Da Nang Air Base, the commanding officer of A Company, 3rd Tank Battalion, 9th MEB (*pointing*), gives instructions to his tank commanders on the impact area of a planned firing exercise on May 1, 1965. At this point, there was not a specifically designed role for Marine armor, and these types of exercises were essential to maintain a high state of readiness.

After moving into position for the firing exercise, Marines of A Company, 3rd Tank Battalion, unload ammo from one M48A3 in order that it is distributed to the rest of the tanks. A clean tarp has been carefully laid on the ground to keep the rounds free of dirt that could cause issues during the firing process.

Under the watchful eyes of an armed helicopter, unloading continues at Hoi-Dong-Xa beach in early May 1965. This equipment is being used in the construction of a SATS airfield at Chu Lai. "Short Airfield for Tactical Support" (SATS) was a concept designed to meet Marine Corps requirements for the rapid construction of tactical airfields—essentially shore-based carrier decks. Although the eventual field at Chu Lai would not qualify as short, it would make use of SATS components, including catapults and arresting gear.

By early June, Marines were aggressively patrolling the areas north and northwest of the airbase in order to engage the Viet Cong. Operations were also underway to relocate civilians out of what had become a true combat zone. Here, a patrol negotiates one of the numerous small streams that cross the region. Their armament and equipment are a marked contrast to that seen later in the conflict.

Brig. Gen. Keith B. McCutcheon, commanding general, 3rd Marine Air Wing (*right*), and former secretary of the Army Robert Stevens (*left*) discuss the current tactical situation under a HAWK missile launcher at the Da Nang airfield with an unidentified Marine captain on June 22, 1965. The HAWK system was designed to defend against low-flying enemy aircraft—a threat that never materialized at Da Nang.

The new operational airstrip at Chu Lai became home to both helicopter and Marine fixed-wing squadrons. Three A-4 Skyhawk squadrons, VMA-225, VMA-311, and VMA-214, made up the aircraft group. As part of the humanitarian effort associated with their deployment, the Marine aviators conducted a clothing distribution to the villagers in the Chu Lai area on June 22, 1965.

A Marine from Delta Company, 1st Battalion, 9th Marines, keeps a close eye on a village hut during a search-and-clear operation held on June 27, 1965, approximately 13 miles northwest of Da Nang Air Base. The operation was the first held by this battalion since its arrival in Vietnam on June 16. His gear is typical of this time period, being composed of elements of the USMC M1941 pack system.

Two Marines discuss their Ontos combat vehicle with their commanding officer, Maj. Gen. Lewis W. Walt, during the general's visit to the Chu Lai perimeter on July 10, 1965. Officially known as "Rifle, Multiple 106 mm, Self-Propelled, M50," the Ontos was a light armored, tracked vehicle designed to give USMC units a reliable and easy-to-use antitank platform. It mounted six 106 mm manually loaded M40A1C recoilless rifles in two arrays of three rifles and a centrally mounted .30-caliber.

After returning from a resupply mission on July 28, 1965, Marine Medium Helicopter Squadron (HMM) 261 UH-34Ds line up at the fuel station before parking their helicopters at the Da Nang Air Base. Sikorsky's radial-powered UH-34 helicopter was the workhorse of the USMC at this time. Its Wright R-1820-84 engine had significant power, and the machine had a capacity of sixteen fully laden Marines in addition to its crew of two.

The substantial bulk of an LVTP-5A1 of B Company, 3rd Amtrac Battalion, rolls past walking Marines on August 13, 1965. The Marines are from H Company, 2nd Battalion, 3rd Marines, who were conducting a sweep-and-clear operation along the Ca De Son River. The LVTP-5A1 was excellent for providing armored transportation from the water to the beachhead but soon became unpopular for sustained ground operations due to its propensity to burn.

PFC Stephan L. Brown of Wellsville, Ohio, places a round into his crew's 105 mm howitzer on August 30, 1965. This marked the 10,000th round fired by Battery B, 12th Marines, since they landed in Vietnam earlier that year. The 105 mm M101A1 howitzer was a redesignation of the World War II M2A1 howitzer, and many of the pieces used by the USMC at this time were wartime veterans.

Helicopters prepare to lift off the flight deck of the amphibious assault ship USS *Iwo Jima* (LPH-2) during Operation Dagger Thrust in October 1965. The objective of this operation was to use the substantial naval and amphibious capabilities available to conduct a series of rapid and narrow thrusts into the countryside to surprise and disrupt Viet Cong activity. Preparations were generally made under the cover of darkness, with raids commencing at sunrise.

The lumbering bulk of a Sikorsky CH-37C Mojave fills the background of this shot of a refueling operation on October 8, 1965. Marine airstrips used the TAFDS (Temporary Airfield Fuel Dispensing System), a system of large rubber bladders to store the fuel, with hoses and portable pumps to deliver it.

Marines of F Company, 2nd Battalion, 7th Marines, move toward an incoming UH-34D helicopter during Operation Blue Marlin on November 11, 1965. Operation Blue Marlin was a combined USMC/VNMC movement conducted between Chu Lai and Tam Ky and began on November 7. BLT 2/7 was airlifted to amphibious shipping from its former TAOR at Qui Nhon to Chu Lai, where it combined with the 3rd Battalion, Vietnamese Marine Corps.

Marines of E Company, 2nd Battalion, 9th Marines, are being resupplied by helicopter during Operation Harvest Moon on December 10, 1965. This operation had begun in the Que Son valley as an engagement between ARVN units and the 1st Viet Cong Regiment. The 1st Battalion, 5th ARVN Regiment, and 11th ARVN Ranger Battalion had hoped to conduct a decisive battle with the VC unit but were ambushed on December 9. USMC units were quickly called in to assist.

Marines of G Company, 2nd Battalion, 9th Marines, under fire while attacking Hill 251 during Operation Harvest Moon on December 12. By this date, a major engagement was underway, and fighting had shifted to the nearby Phuoc Ha valley in pursuit of fleeing VC units. The valley was the site of no fewer than two tactical strikes by B-52s during the intensified fighting. All the Marines in this shot wear elements of the USMC M1941 pack system, as befitting units on extended field missions.

Landing Zone Oak was established to funnel supplies and reinforcements into the battle area. An M50A1 Ontos is seen here on December 17, 1965. A few were sent in to provide security for the temporary base. By this point, monsoon rains had begun covering the region, creating wet and chilly conditions for the troops. A large tarp covered the porous gun mount of the Ontos, and the Marines on board sport their ponchos.

Adm. U. S. Grant Sharp, commander in chief, Pacific, talks with Lt. Col. David Clements, commanding officer of 2nd Battalion, 3rd Marines, about the protection of the village of Le My, about 10 miles northwest of Da Nang. Adm. Sharp was a distant relative of president and Civil War general Ulysses S. Grant, who had married Sharp's grandmother's sister. Lt. Col. Clements personifies the 1960s Marine here, with his M1941 pack system suspenders, Cotton Sateen Utility Uniform, and Leaf Pattern Camouflage Helmet Cover. An M18 smoke grenade hangs from his map case.

An M48A3 of B Company, 3rd Tank Battalion, guards the perimeter near Hoa Long village. This photo illustrates one of the biggest maintenance headaches for Marine tankers deployed in the coastal areas of Vietnam: fine sand. It was a constant source of aggravation, working its way into all areas of the suspension and tracks. Drive sprockets, which were normally reversed twice a year, were sometimes reversed daily to prevent differential wear.

A Marine M38A1 drives along the perimeter of the Da Nang Air Base. Another M38A1 and an M422 Mighty Mite can be seen behind it. At this time, both vehicles were considered interim designs and would later be replaced with the ubiquitous M151 series of quarter-ton tactical trucks. The new trucks started appearing in the USMC inventory early in 1966.

An LVTP-5A1 is seen here disgorging troops and equipment after a sweep. Most of the Marines present in the photo wear the M55 flak vest. Known officially as "Armor, Body, Fragmentation, Protective: Upper Torso," this vest was an improvement over the M1952A model, which was also still in widespread use at this time. Interestingly, several of the Marines have attached elements of their pack system to a packboard to more evenly distribute those loads. This item was commonly used to transport mortar and bazooka rounds.

Marines of F Company, 2nd Battalion, 4th Regiment, pass by an LVTP5A1 after landing on the beach during opening phases of Operation Double Eagle, January 28, 1966. This combined Marine, US Army, and ARVN operation was designed as a giant sweep of Quang Ngai Province in an attempt to engage the NVA/VC in open battle. The corresponding Army designation was Operation Masher; Air Force units also participated. It was to be the largest amphibious landing since Inchon in 1950 and involved over 5,000 Marines.

CHAPTER 2
1966–1967

US Marine 1Lt. J. R. Schwartz, Columbus, Ohio, advisor to the Black Panther Company, 1st Division, accompanied his unit into battle seven miles north of Hue. Eighteen rebels were killed in the village of Hien An and twelve were taken captive. US Marine and Army choppers landed the unit under Viet Cong automatic weapons fire. *Official USMC Photo by WO Rob Robinson*

In 1966, Carlos Hathcock was deployed to Vietnam, assigned to base security. Hathcock soon volunteered for sniper training. His exploits soon became legendary. Although the regulations of the time required that a confirmed sniper kill had to be observed by an officer, and not the sniper's spotter, Hathcock nevertheless tallied eighty-five kills in thirteen months. Discharged in 1967, he rejoined and redeployed a week later and racked up eight more kills before being badly burned rescuing fellow Marines from a damaged amphibious tractor. His own estimate, reflecting the lack of the presence of an observing officer, would put his total at 300–400, enough that the North Vietnamese put the unheard-of bounty of $30,000 on Hathcock (other Marine snipers warranted only a $2,000 bounty).

The July 2, 1967, ambush of the 1st Battalion, 9th Marines, 2 miles northwest of Con Thien made that date the bloodiest day of the war for the Marines, with eighty-four riflemen killed, and resulted in the unit being given the moniker "the Walking Dead." Beyond this battle, it is also worthwhile to mention that this unit had the longest sustained combat (and highest killed-in-action rate) in Marine Corps history, as a result of being in combat in Vietnam for forty-seven months and seven days, with 26 percent of the men passing through the unit being killed in action.

Despite the aggressive attacks by the North, with the aid of the 1st Marine Air Wing, Marine tanks, and grit the Marines held Con Thien, although at the cost of 340 Marines killed and 3,086 wounded.

In 1967, Gen. Cushman replaced Gen. Walt, and a series of amphibious operations were launched along the coast, particularly in Quang Nam Province.

Marine Corps tanks were not significantly engaged in Operation Double Eagle but continued to train during that period. This M67A2 flame tank shoots a rod of flame during a demonstration in January. The M67A2 was the final flame tank manufactured for the US military and was nearly identical to the standard M48A3, on which it was based. They were normally assigned to the Headquarters and Service Company as a flame section of nine tanks parceled in groups of three.

Three M109 155 mm howitzers of M Battery, 4th Battalion, 12th Regiment, move into position 3 miles south of Phu Bai before firing in support of Operation Double Eagle. The M109 was relatively new in the USMC inventory at this time. Lightweight and highly mobile, the M109 had an M126 155 mm gun in an M127 howitzer mount. It carried twenty-eight rounds of ammunition and also mounted a .50-caliber machine gun, seen within its protective canvas cover on the middle vehicle.

Although significant contact eluded most Marine units during Operation Double Eagle, there was some combat. This lance corporal takes up a sitting position in a small defilade on January 29, 1966. He is firing the venerable M14, the standard rifle of the USMC at the time. The automatic M14 fired 7.62 mm ball ammunition and was popular with the troops due to its twenty-round clip, stopping power, and accuracy. Its eventual replacement by the M16 was largely due to the M14's substantial weight of 11.22 pounds.

An LVTP-5A1 being turned around in the well deck of the USS *Alamo* (LSD-33) following Operation Osage in April 1966. The vehicle appears much like a boat in this shot, and its performance in the water was sound. When completely buttoned up, it could even endure a rollover. An air-cooled gasoline Continental V12 powered the LVTP-5A1, and it shared a transmission with the M48. Two large cargo doors in the top of the hull helped facilitate waterborne loading. The two 55-gallon drums lashed to the top hull are of interest.

Marines of Battalion Landing Team 1/5 board the aerial assault helicopters from the deck of an amphibious assault ship, USS *Princeton* (LPH-5), during Operation Osage. As one of the 7th Fleet's Special Landing Forces, use of the BLT was at the discretion of the fleet commander. Consequently, they were often used at this time as a quick-reaction force, as in this instance where they were landing in the hills near the DMZ in an attempt to interdict NVA elements. The Marine nearest the camera uses a packboard to carry comm wire and what appears to be a mortar sight in its protective box, as well as his personal gear.

Two Ontos are moving along a railroad track in the area north of Chu Lai on April 9, 1966, during Operation Iowa. This search-and-destroy operation was conducted by the 3rd Battalion, 1st Marines, and 2nd Battalion, 4th Marines, in Quang Tin Province. The primary drawbacks of the Ontos as a support weapon were the necessity to reload the rifles from outside the vehicle, and its light armor. In fact, the US Army had rejected the entire run of vehicles largely due to those factors.

Marines of the 1st Battalion, 7th Regiment, descend into a rice paddy to board waiting UH-34D helicopters during Operation Nevada on April 15, 1966. Also known as Operation Lien Ket, this was a multiple-unit search-and-destroy operation involving the 1st Battalion, 2nd Marines; 2nd Battalion, 7th Marines; the ARVN 2nd Division; and the VNMC. As search-and-destroy missions became more elaborate and lengthy, individual load requirements were raised considerably.

Lt. Col. Leon Utter, commanding officer of 2nd Battalion, 7th Marines; Maj. Gen. Lewis J. Fields, commanding general of 1st Marine Division; and Col. Eugene Haffey, commanding officer of 7th Marines, discuss the results of Operation Nevada in Chau Thuan village with an unidentified officer on April 16, 1966. Both the First and Second Pattern Jungle Fatigue Coats are seen here, as well as the Cotton Sateen OG-107 fatigues worn by Maj. Gen. Fields.

Ontos and troops of G Company, 2nd Battalion, 7th Marine Regiment, are on the line, preparing to sweep through Lac Son village in Quang Ngai Province on July 29, 1966. Although originally arranged as an antitank company of twenty vehicles within the MEB, the Ontos were eventually broken up into smaller groups for greater utility. Gradually, their role as fire support vehicles was taken over by Marine M48A3s. The Marine on the far right carries an M3A1 .45-caliber submachine gun, a weapon still issued to Marine armored crewmen at this time.

Cpl. Charles Gutierrez, a grenadier of G Company, 2nd Battalion, 5th Marine Regiment, displays a crude device used like a bell to warn the Viet Cong of approaching Marines on August 28, 1966. The bell consists of a fin assembly and canister of an 81 mm illumination round. The corporal led the patrol that found the bell near the hamlet of Ky Sanh, northwest of Chu Lai, Vietnam.

Men of A Company, 1st Battalion, 7th Marine Regiment, move on a frontal sweep through rice paddies to a fortified village, supposedly occupied by the Viet Cong. The action took place south of Quang Ngai during Operation Golden Fleece on September 22, 1966. The 1st Battalion of 7th Marines and the ARVN 4th Regiment conducted this operation in order to protect that season's rice harvest. Each Marine carries a substantial amount of additional ammunition.

A 105 mm howitzer of B Battery, 1st Battalion, 12th Marines, firing from Hill 41 on September 30, 1966, in support of Operation Golden Fleece. Their piece has been dubbed "Suddenly," and like many fixed artillery positions in Vietnam, it sits within a meticulously prepared revetment composed of sandbags and carefully positioned Marsten matting. Six guns made up a typical battery.

Marines of M Battery, 3rd Battalion, 12th Marines, prepare to fire their 155 mm howitzer at Viet Cong positions from the artillery plateau about 8 miles northwest of Dong Ha on October 24, 1966. A crewman is setting fuses on the 155 mm rounds in the left foreground. The towed 155 mm howitzer, used by both the Army and the Marine Corps in Vietnam, was a direct descendant of the World War II M1 howitzer, being redesignated M114 in 1962.

An M109 155 mm self-propelled howitzer of M Company, 3rd Battalion, 12th Regiment, fires toward enemy positions at Phu Bai, Republic of Vietnam, on October 25 1966. A substantial amount of ammunition stands ready in the foreground, and empty shell casings litter the area to the right. The US Army fielded a 105 mm version of the M109 in Vietnam, known as the M108. Most were later converted to the more useful M109 configuration.

At this point in the conflict, Marine armor was still frequently called upon to provide base and perimeter security, as is the case with the M48A3 standing watch over Marine Aircraft Group 36 at Ky Ha on November 18, 1966. The original caption points out that the individual in the commander's hatch is actually an aviator. This M48A3 lacks the distinctive round vision block beneath the cupola of the Model B and also mounts the earlier, circular Crouse-Hinds searchlight. A deep-wading snorkel has been mounted on the right side of the turret.

These Seabees are laying interlocking steel mat at Ky Ha, Vietnam, on Christmas Day 1966. In the background, UH-34Ds of the Marine Aircraft Group 36 refuel. Note the winch on the port side of the nearest helicopter. It is mounted on a frame structure in order to clear the doors. These aircraft served for a surprisingly long period of time with the USMC in Vietnam, before being gradually phased out in favor of the CH-53 and the CH-46.

A Marine 105 mm gun crew of B Company, 1st Battalion, 11th Marine Regiment, check their gun over in preparation for any fire missions that may be called in. These crewmen appear to be admirers of their World War II brethren, wearing the older "frog skin" helmet covers, which are even present on those stowed in the background. The gun commander also appears to be wearing an M41 field jacket. Only the presence of M14 rifles in the rack at the rear of the revetment reveals the time period.

A CH-37C helicopter lifts a damaged UH-34D helicopter that was mortared when it came to resupply the men of F Company, 2nd Battalion, 9th Marines. Both the tail rotor and the main rotor have been removed for transport. The ungainly looking CH-37C was the primary heavy-lifting helicopter of the USMC at this time and was frequently used to recover downed aircraft as well as transport artillery pieces. The CH-37C had two large clamshell doors in the front of the fuselage that could encompass loads as large as a quarter-ton truck, but its low clearance made it generally unpopular in this role.

Unusually, all five members of this Marine gun crew wear their M55 body armor. Counter battery fire was not very common at this time in the conflict, but it could still occur—especially from mortars. The gun commander is standing by with his headset and microphone to receive instructions from the battery commander, and a crewman stands by with a round to the rear of the gun. The original caption states that this howitzer was once fired on Iwo Jima in World War II.

SMaj. Herbert J. Sweet and LCpl. Ebner Travis examine the sighting mechanism of their 105 mm M101A1 howitzer in January 1967. Officially known as "Telescope, Panoramic, M12A2" and "Mount, Telescope, M12A1," great care was always taken to ensure that this part of the gun remained in peak operational form. It appears that the sergeant major is wearing his M43 field jacket on this overcast January day, no doubt a relic of his service in either World War II or Korea.

During a visit to Vietnam on January 12, 1967, local political and military leaders escorted the undersecretary of the Navy, Robert H. B. Baldwin, and Maj. Gen. H. Nickerson Jr. on a guided tour of Hoa Quang Refugee Resettlement Center. Undersecretary Baldwin (center) wears a pressed set of Cotton Sateen OG-107 fatigues, while Maj. Gen. Nickerson (right) wears a pressed example of the First Pattern Jungle Fatigue Coat, as evidenced by the exposed buttons.

Lt. Cmdr. Glenn Ford, USN, scouts locations for the Navy promotional documentary *Global Marine* in one of Da Nang's busy market places on January 20, 1967. The popular actor had originally joined the Marine Corps Reserve in 1942 (after a brief stint in the US Coast Guard), eventually being medically discharged in 1944. Reenlisting in the Naval Reserve in 1958, he continued using his celebrity for the benefit of the service until his retirement in the 1970s as a captain.

This Marine is waiting for assistance to pull a mired M151 from a rice paddy during Operation Deckhouse VI. This was a two-phase search-and-destroy operation involving the 1st Battalion of 4th Marines and HMM-363 held in February 1967. The vehicle appears to be brand new at this point and still retains the plywood protective cover for the windshield used for amphibious operations. Snorkel equipment is lashed to the structure, as well. This M151 has a radio mount and antenna on the left side.

Marines of E Company 2/9 prepare to board UH-34D helicopters during soggy weather on February 5, 1967. They will be airlifted into a blocking-force position for an ARVN Black Panther unit making a sweep in the Royal Tombs area about 10 miles south of Hue. Full packs, flak vests, and extra bandoliers of ammunition are all in evidence in anticipation of heavy contact.

An M60 machine gunner and his assistant from A Company, 2nd Platoon, 1st Battalion, 9th Marines, fires at Viet Cong fleeing through a rice paddy during Operation Chinook II on February 21, 1967. The 15-pound M122 tripod in use here is seldom seen in photos, unless the gun is being used in a fixed position. With the weapon's high rate of fire, its use would no doubt greatly improve accuracy at long distances.

An M76 Otter amphibious vehicle from Headquarters and Service Company, 3rd Motor Transport Battalion, climbs over a rice paddy dike while delivering supplies to C Company, 1st Battalion, 9th Marines, during Operation Chinook II on February 22, 1967. Conceived as a replacement for the World War II–era M29 Weasel, the Otter's pneumatic tires and wide tracks were ideal for the rice paddies and soft ground of Vietnam. Although not a combat vehicle, it was frequently equipped with a ring mount for a .50-caliber machine gun.

Tired Marines of A Company, 1st Battalion, 9th Marines, rest after completing Operation Chinook II. They are waiting to be airlifted into Cam Lo Province to begin an interdiction operation to be conducted approximately 1 mile south of the Demilitarized Zone on February 28, 1967. The weather had turned somewhat cold on that day, as evidenced by the long sleeves and jackets on the assembled group.

Sunny weather has returned for these Marines of the 4th Regiment as they move through a stream in search of North Vietnamese soldiers during Operation Beacon Hill, approximately 3 miles west of Cam Lo, in March 1967. This operation began on March 20 and continued through April 3. Over 330 enemy dead were claimed during the course of the engagement. The nearest Marine has obtained a set of Army-issued second-pattern M1956 suspenders for his personal gear.

PFC Brian O'Connell of Quebec, Canada, prepares to chamber a round into his 105 mm M101A1 howitzer on March 20, 1967. This round was the 75,000th to be fired by C Battery, 1st Battalion, 12th Regiment. Pvt. O'Connell wears a well-cared-for set of Cotton Sateen fatigues imprinted with the Marine Corps logo. Around the back of the revetment, M55 flak vests stand ready for use on specially constructed stands.

In accordance with Marine doctrine of the time, maximum use was made of the Corps' amphibious capabilities to place large assets on the ground in order to swiftly engage enemy units. The dock landing ship USS *Monticello* (LSD-35) launches LVTP-5A1s and other amphibious craft loaded with Marines and their gear during the opening phases of Operation Beacon Hill I on March 20, 1967. They will land south of the Demilitarized Zone in Quang Tri Province.

Members of the 1st Amphibian Tractor Battalion ride on a patrol on March 24, 1967, during Operation Perry. Their mounts are the somewhat rare LVTE-1 (Landing Vehicle, Tracked, Engineer). The LVTE-1 was an LVTP-5 with a large mine-clearing blade that was capable of clearing a 3.7-meter-wide path to a depth of 0.41 meters. Plastic buoyancy modules installed in the hull helped compensate for the blade when in the water. The rack on the top hull held an explosive line charge. Only forty-one units were built.

A CH-53A helicopter airlifts a 12,000-pound M114 155 mm howitzer from Duc Pho, where it was supporting the 7th Marines near Quang Ngai on March 30, 1967. The Sikorsky CH-53 Sea Stallion was brand new at this time, having just entered service with the USMC in January 1967. Designed as a replacement for the piston engine UH-34D and CH-37C, this turboshaft machine would end up serving for decades.

A Marine from K Company, 4th Battalion, 11th Marines, attaches a steel cable to another M114 155 mm howitzer in preparation for a lift by a CH-53 Sea Stallion helicopter. The howitzer will be transported from Chu Lai to Nui Dang during Operation DeSoto in support of the 7th Marines on March 30, 1967. In preparation for its journey, the howitzer's gun travel lock is in place, as well as its barrel cover.

LCpl. Robert A. Gazaille endures yet another 90-degree search-and-destroy operation 12 miles south of Da Nang on May 14, 1967. Gazaille is a member of Company C, 1st Battalion, 1st Marine Regiment. At about this time, the Marine Corps began experimenting with replacing the M14 with the new M16 rifle. The design of the flash suppressor on the weapon seen here indicates that it is an XM16E1, an experimental and improved version of the original. Details of the M55 flak vest, such as its stubby collar, are clearly visible here.

A maintenance crew from Marine Medium Helicopter Squadron 165 rigs a hoist sling to a downed CH-46 Sea Knight helicopter on May 12, 1967. Its pilot had landed the helicopter in a river northwest of Chu Lai after enemy rounds had set it on fire. By landing in the river, the pilot extinguished the flames. The Boeing CH-46 had gradually come into Marine Corps service in 1961, and like the CH-53, it was intended as a replacement for the aging fleet of UH-34 helicopters.

Marine first lieutenant Berry C. Bunch, twenty-three, from Chester, California, takes off on his first combat mission in Vietnam on May 24, 1967. The F-4B Phantom pilot flew with Marine Fighter Attack Squadron 115, which had returned to Vietnam that month.

An M422A1 Mighty Mite sits in the foreground of this view of the headquarters area of the newly dedicated Camp Paul O. Evans on June 27, 1967. This was the regimental headquarters of the 4th Marines. An interesting field expedient is visible in the right background. An aircraft drop tank has been used to create a reservoir for a shower that has been attached to a latrine. A tarp provides a measure of privacy.

The view from a convoy as it approaches Camp Evans, also on June 27. The base is visible in the background. The camp was named after LCpl. Paul Evans of the Marines, who had been killed during Operation Chinook. A row of M422A1 Mighty Mites sits to the left, along with several quarter-ton M416B1 trailers. The M416B1, produced for use with M422-series vehicles, can be distinguished from the common M416 by the former's use of Mighty Mite wheels and jerry can brackets on the sides of the body. M54 5-ton cargo trucks can be seen in the distance.

Marines of the 3rd Battalion, 9th Marine Regiment, dash to a waiting CH-46 helicopter at Dong Ha. Part of the battalion-size reaction force, they were en route to reinforce the 1st Battalion, 9th Marines, battling North Vietnamese army forces at Con Thien, south of the DMZ, on July 2, 1967. This photo was likely taken during Operation Bear Bite, held at that time. This is a mortar section, with the third man from the left carrying the tube, while others to his left carry the tripod and baseplate on packboards.

A landing craft utility (LCU) moving a 3rd Tank Battalion tank up the Dong Ha River for unloading on July 6, 1967. Occasionally, Marine tankers would raise their M48s on landing craft by using large timbers. This would allow them to fire over the sides of the craft and create an ad hoc gunboat. This may be the case here, since the top of the track return run is visible. Marines typically referred to LCUs as "U-boats."

Lt. Col. L. R. Roper, commanding officer of the 1st Battalion, 40th Artillery (*left*); Capt. J. L. Crosby, commanding officer of A Battery, 40th Artillery; and Col. W. R. Morrison, commanding officer of 12th Marines, celebrate the 150,000th round to be fired by the unit on July 11, 1967, as they stand in front of one of the unit's M109 self-propelled howitzers. All wear the second-pattern Jungle Fatigue Coat, as evidenced by the hidden buttons. The official nomenclature was Jungle Fatigue Coat, Man's, Combat, Tropical DSA 100-1387.

Marines of B Company, 1st Battalion, 4th Marines, and the tanks of the 3rd Tank Battalion team up together during Operation Hickory II on July 15, 1967. This operation also utilized SLF A and the 2nd Battalion, 3rd Marines. This was the first large search-and-destroy mission into the area south of the DMZ, in order to sweep and clear the area of enemy fortifications and mortar and artillery positions. Marine armor was essential for this task in providing fire support for the infantry.

Marines of the 2nd Battalion, 9th Marine Regiment, return down a trail and through the perimeter of the 3rd Battalion, 4th Marine Regiment, from two days of fierce fighting with North Vietnamese army troops that took place within the Demilitarized Zone during Operation Kingfisher on July 29, 1967. This massive operation was part of a series of engagements that blended into one another over the summer. This was in keeping with Gen. Westmoreland's desire to confront the NVA in direct combat. Officially, Kingfisher resulted in over 1,100 enemy dead.

An M107 175 mm gun of A Battery, 2nd Battalion, 94th Artillery, fires a round in support of Marines in the A Shau valley during Operation Pike on August 1, 1967. The 94th Artillery was an Army unit that had been assigned to the 12th Marine Artillery Regiment since 1966. They brought their brand-new M107 self-propelled guns, greatly increasing the firepower of the unit. Entering service in 1962, the M107 had a maximum range of 25 miles, and a good crew could sustain a rate of fire of one round per minute. It shared a chassis with the M110 203 mm SPG.

Commandant of the Marine Corps, Gen. Wallace M. Greene Jr., discusses military tactics used in Vietnam on August 10, 1967, with Army general William C. Westmoreland, commanding general of Military Assistance Command, Vietnam. Listening to the discussion is Lt. Gen. Robert E. Cushman Jr., commanding general of III Marine Amphibious Force. Tragically, Westmoreland never warmed to the Marine Corps' often-successful efforts at pacification, favoring a blunt application of American firepower whenever possible.

Marines fight a fuel fire started by an enemy rocket attack on the Dong Ha Combat Base on August 28, 1967. This was one of three separate attacks by the NVA that took place starting on August 26. Some 150 artillery and rocket projectiles hit the base during that period. Two helicopters belonging to HMM-361 were destroyed and twenty-four others were damaged in the attack.

Marines of 1st Battalion, 7th Regiment, mug for the camera on board an LVTP-5A1 on September 8, 1967. They are departing for Operation Yazoo, which took place 12 miles west of Da Nang in Happy Valley. The operation also included the 3rd Battalion, 11th Marines. The area west of Da Nang was an area of nearly constant enemy activity, and the continuing operations there caused the Marines to ironically dub it "Happy Valley."

The crew of an LVTC-5A1, the command version of the LVTP-5A1, prepare for a sweep during Operation Swift in September 1967. This search-and-destroy operation was conducted in the Que Son valley from September 12 to 16, by Task Force X-Ray. This varied unit was composed of the 1st Battalion, 5th Marines; 3rd Battalion, 5th Marines; 2nd Battalion, 11th Marines; the ARVN 21st, 37th, and Ranger Battalions; the 3rd Battalion, ARVN 4th Regiment; and the 3rd Battalion, ARVN 6th Regiment.

Marines of E Company, 2nd Battalion, 1st Marine Regiment, vector in a landing UH-34D helicopter during Operation Shelbyville on September 29, 1967. Additional units deployed during this operation were the 1st Battalion, 3rd Marines; the 3rd Battalion, 5th Marines; and 1st Battalion, 11th Marines. Operation Shelbyville was a search-and-destroy mission held 25 miles south of Da Nang.

Cpl. Donald M. Ward, an M48A3 driver with C Company, 1st Tank Battalion, scans the muddy road while providing security for a convoy near Da Nang. Monsoon rains had turned roads near Da Nang into a virtual quagmire on this October day in 1967. The three forward periscopes of the M48 provided very limited visibility for the driver, so he often rode exposed from his hatch—or even standing up. This photo provides a good view of his microphone array.

This Marine, an operator with Otter Platoon, 1st Marines, keeps a watchful eye at the helm of his ring-mounted .50-caliber machine gun on October 18, 1967. He wears the M1952A flak jacket, easily recognizable by the absence of a collar and its distinctive epaulets. This photo was taken during Operation Onslow, a multiple-unit engagement composed of the 2nd Platoon, C Company, 1st Marine Division; the 1st Battalion, 5th Marine Regiment; and the ARVN 2nd Ranger Battalion.

Marine artillerymen of the 2nd Battalion, 12th Marines, at Con Thien pound the North Vietnamese in the Demilitarized Zone with high-explosive and white phosphorus shells from their M101A1 105 mm howitzer on October 19, 1967. Helicopters of the 1st Marine Aircraft Wing supplied ammunition, which is consumed virtually around the clock. This was all in support of Operation Formation Leader, a "heliborne" and amphibious search-and-destroy operation held in the coastal region east of Route 9 that was conducted by the 2nd Battalion, 3rd Marines.

Supplies await disposition in a corner of the Naval Support Activity at Da Nang in November 1967. Naval craft line the waterfront in the background. Refined during the Second World War and perfected in the ensuing Cold War, the American military logistics machine was a materiel juggernaut by the 1960s. Da Nang was the logistic center of USMC operations for their entire time in Vietnam. The immediate region offered many superb, sheltered anchorages due to its location on a small peninsula at the mouth of the Han River estuary.

The chilly, wet weather of an early Vietnam winter is in evidence with this Ontos crew on November 25, 1967. The crew and their weapon are entrenched near Con Thein and are part of Operation Ballistic Arch, a combined helicopter and amphibious assault operation held about 4 miles south of the DMZ in Quang Tri Province by the 1st Battalion, 3rd Marines. Both crew members wear hooded waterproof jackets under their flak vests.

The air tower at Khe Sanh Airbase on the afternoon of November 29, 1967. The area around the base had been the scene of fierce fighting the previous spring. The base was first established as a Special Forces camp in 1962 near the village that bears its name. Although not evident in this black-and-white photo, the boards surrounding the enclosure were painted red with gold lettering. The placard indicates that Marine Air Traffic Control Unit 62 is in charge of landing operations. A USMC garrison had joined the Army one in 1966.

Seabees of Mobile Construction Battalion (MCB) 301 set and seal runway mats into place at Khe Sanh on the same day as the previous photo. Strategically located approximately 14 miles south of the DMZ to the north and just 6 miles from the Laotian border to the west, Khe Sanh was considered a significant location in thwarting the movement of NVA assets into South Vietnam. Increased enemy activity at this time had caused the base to be expanded and improved. The location was to gain special significance in the coming months.

Marines of the 106 mm Recoilless Rifle platoon test the range of their weapon on December 10, 1967. The M40 was actually 105 mm in bore; the 106 mm designation was applied in order to distinguish it from the earlier 105 mm M27 weapon. A .50-caliber spotting rifle was installed in brackets at the top of the weapon, and its trajectory was intended to match that of the larger gun. The one-piece shells were issued in HEAT, HEAP, HEP, and Canister. It had an effective firing range of about 1,350 meters or 1,480 yards.

A Marine of the 81 mm mortars, 2nd Battalion, 7th Marines, is wet and cold as he takes a standing break during Operation Pitt, held in December 1967, approximately 12 miles north of Da Nang. A clear view of his XM16E1 is provided here. Its forward grip bears a resemblance to the original M16, but the duckbill flash suppressor and forward assist (*above the trigger*) reveals that this is the modified version. Initially very unpopular due to the extremely erroneous assumption that it was self-cleaning, the M16A1 was to become the standard rifle for all US ground forces in 1969.

A Pettibone all-terrain forklift comes to the back of a Marine KC-130F to lift off cargo at the Dong Ha airfreight facility. The forklift lacks the typical Roll Over Protective Structure (ROPS) for the operator—an essential piece of equipment for preventing injury during the process of loading and unloading. Dong Ha Combat Base was an extensive USMC logistical hub located off Route 1 about halfway between Hue City and the DMZ.

Men of the 2nd Battalion, 26th Marines, rush to board a waiting CH-46 from Marine Medium Helicopter Squadron 364. Responsible for the protection of the northern half of the Da Nang Rocket Belt, the Marines are responding to a possible enemy sighting. The CH-46 Sea Knight could carry up to twenty-five Marines and their kit. It appears that additional troops are waiting to the rear of the aircraft to join the fourteen that are rushing onto the ramp.

The M67A2 Flamethrower tank was based on the M48A3, and the flamethrower itself was designed to mimic a conventional 90 mm gun barrel. The flame unit was known as M7A1-6, and it was further composed of the M7 fuel and pressure system and the M6 flame gun. Tanks inside the turret were used to store the fuel for the flamethrower. A logistics "tail" was required for sustained operation of the weapon, with a fuel truck and other support vehicles. One shot of flame was known as a "rod."

The boatlike front hull of the M76 Otter is clearly seen in this three-quarter view of the vehicle. The M76 used unique metal and plastic tracks that constituted nearly two-thirds of its width. The cleverly integrated offset pneumatic road wheels (eight per side) not only aided in flotation but also made for a very smooth ride. Its primary drawback was that its high silhouette made it difficult to conceal. Additionally, its long service life—it had been in use since the early 1950s—eventually lead to its replacement by the M116A1 Husky.

On January 20, 1968, a Marine patrol near Khe Sanh encountered a large North Vietnamese force. The next day the enemy began bombarding Khe Sanh, taking the area under siege. The Marines' main ammunition storage was destroyed in this shelling. The siege of Khe Sanh lasted seventy-seven days and, like the protracted siege of Con Thien before it, also involved the 1st Battalion, 9th Marines. The official casualty figures for Khe Sanh are 205 killed and 1,667 wounded, but if the relief effort and the attack on the nearby Special Forces camp are included, it swells to 703 dead, 2,642 wounded, and seven missing in action.

The attack on Khe Sanh was a precursor to the Tết Offensive. Tết, the Vietnamese celebration of the lunar new year, had traditionally been a day of informal truce in Vietnam, but that was not to be the case in 1968. With Khe Sahn occupying the minds of American military and political leaders, North Vietnamese general Vo Nguyen Giap attacked thirteen South Vietnamese cities in the early hours of January 30. Within twenty-four hours, the number of attacks had reached 120. Included in the targets were the US embassy in Saigon and the city of Huế.

Huế was the ancient capital of Vietnam and, as such, was the home of many historic sites, including the Citadel, which surrounds the former imperial capital. In the early morning of January 31, 1968, roughly a division-sized force of People's Army of Vietnam and Việt Cộng attacked Huế. Fewer than 100 US troops, including Marines, were in the city, which was largely garrisoned by a small ARVN force. The largest Marine contingent was at the Phu Bai Combat Base, 7 miles south on Highway 1, which was subjected to rocket and mortar attack at roughly the same time Huế was attacked.

Included in the attack on Huế was a heavy assault on the small MACV compound. The MACV defenders held, allowing the compound to serve as a base of operations.

Lacking a clear picture of what was going on in Huế, the Marines from Phu Bai began moving up the highway to the ancient capital, encountering increasing fire en route. As a result of actions during the fight toward Huế, GSgt. John L. Canley and Sgt. Alfredo Cantu Gonzalez were awarded the Medal of Honor, the latter posthumously.

Although initially hamstrung by orders not to use heavy weapons for fear of damaging culturally significant or historic structures, as the French had done in 1947, ultimately the Marines were able to claw their way back into the city. Facing the seriousness of the situation, authorities finally relented, and artillery began to be used, in particular recoilless rifles. Finally, the Marines and allies prevailed, but it was hard fought—the longest battle of the Tết Offensive, beginning January 31, and mopping-up operations were declared finished on March 2, 1968.

The next month the enemy launched another offensive, sometimes called a mini-Tết, attempting to seize the large Marine Corps HQ and logistics base at Dong Ha. Marines of Battalion Landing Team 2/4 stopped elements of two regiments from the 320th North Vietnamese Army at Dai Ho, near Dong Ha. Actions during this battle resulted in Company E commander Capt. James E. Livingston and Company G commander Capt. Jay R. Vargas being awarded the Medal of Honor. In addition to these two men, fifty-six other Marines earned the respect of the nation and the Medal of Honor for heroism in Vietnam.

Gen. Westmoreland was replaced by Gen. Creighton Abrams on June 10, 1968, only a few days after Medal of Honor recipient Maj. Gen. Raymond G. Davis had assumed command of the 3rd Marine Division, relieving Rathvon Tompkins. With the changes in command came a change in strategy, with mobile operations becoming favored over fixed positions. As a result, the hard-fought-for Khe Sanh was ordered abandoned, and the last Marine left on July 5, 1968.

The year would also mark the peak deployment of Marines to Vietnam, with 81,249 of the Corps' 298,498 men being in country. This included twenty-one (of thirty-six) battalions, fourteen fixed-wing air squadrons, and thirteen helicopter squadrons.

Marines of Medium Helicopter Squadron 364 (HMM-364) attempt to extract a CH-46 Sea Knight helicopter that has become stuck in the mud at Phu Bai on January 4, 1968. A small tractor is also assisting. Phu Bai Combat base was located south of Hue City, opposite Highway 1, and had been established by the USMC in 1965. It is sometimes referred to as Camp Hochmuth, after the former commanding general of the 3rd Marine Division, Bruno Hochmuth, who was killed in a helicopter crash north of Hue in November 1967. *National Museum of the United States Marine Corps*

Clean-up continues on the billeting hut of the Headquarters and Service Battalion's Staff NCO area at the Da Nang Air Base on January 7, 1968, after a rocket attack on the second. This was to be the first of the rocket attacks that year, with over thirty rounds falling. After being identified and attacked by the US Air Force, the rocket positions were overrun by Marine patrols. Several dead were found among the remains of Soviet 122 mm rockets and launchers. *National Museum of the United States Marine Corps*

This picturesque overall view of Bru village as seen from Hill 90, just south of the Khe Sanh Airstrip, was taken on January 13, 1968. The Bru were one of Vietnam's many small ethnic subgroups and were known for their distinctive stilted house construction. As the battle for this area heated up over the next two weeks, this area would be evacuated and the quaint structures razed.

Marines of W Battery, 1st Battalion, 13th Marines, clean the barrel of their M114 155 mm howitzer after a fire mission on North Vietnamese positions around Khe Sanh on January 27, 1968. The M114 normally sat raised on a firing jack, a small platform between the front wheels, and it has been lowered for the task of cleaning. Unlike its counterpart, the M101A1 105 mm piece, the 155 mm weapon utilized two-piece ammunition. This required extra care in cleaning the barrel to remove traces of the disintegrating charge.

An M55 8-inch howitzer of 3rd Battalion, 11th Marines, fires during the night of January 31, 1968, in response to the opening phases of the Tet Offensive. This unit was oddly positioned between Hill 327 and the Da Nang base, which meant outgoing rounds passed directly over the heads of other billeted units, making relaxation difficult—to say the least. The M55 was one of the older items in Marine inventory at this time, soon to be phased out by the newer M109 and M107 self-propelled guns.

An LVTH-6A1 provides counter battery fire, also on January 31, 1968. The LVTH-6A1 was the fire support version of the LVTP-5 series. It mounted a 105 mm howitzer on the top of the hull within a rotating turret. A total of 150 rounds could be stored in metal racks installed in the hull, and additional capacity could also be found in the cargo area. The design of the LVTH-6A1 was intended to provide landing Marines with direct fire support on the beachhead. Due to the ever-present mine threat and the presence of Marine armor, once ashore, these vehicles were mostly deployed as self-propelled artillery.

During an infantry sweep south of Khe Sanh, Marines found this hastily abandoned Soviet ZIL-157 5-ton fitter's vehicle. The brand-new truck contained a complete machine shop consisting of a large lathe, hydraulic drill press, and numerous tuning systems. It also had a compressor system, a distillation unit, and an unusual electrical system. This unit was probably intended to be a mobile small-arms repair shop. A great deal of material had been moved down the Ho Chi Minh Trail and stockpiled for the start of the Tet Offensive, and this vehicle was part of that hoard. The slogan on the side refers to the popular 1963 James Bond film. *National Museum of the United States Marine Corps*

An interesting case of enemy ingenuity is pictured here. Third Division Marines captured this unusually modified big-bore weapon during an engagement with the North Vietnamese army near Dong Ha. The weapon had been fashioned from an M79 grenade launcher and is equipped with a fast-draw spring holster made from a cut-down pistol holster. A lanyard has been added to both the holster and the stock of the gun. *National Museum of the United States Marine Corps*

An M48A3 tank attached to the 2nd Battalion, 26th Marines, Special Landing Force, goes ashore during an amphibious training operation at Cua Viet. Taking no chances, the LCU has delivered the tank directly to the sand. The South China Sea was notoriously rough, and the swells often created craters and runnels in the sand close to shore. These had been the cause of several incidents where tanks had been drowned, resulting in extensive recovery operations. This M48A3 has its deep-wading snorkel installed—not a common sight in photos. *National Museum of the United States Marine Corps*

Local workers engage in activities related to the construction of an orphanage on My Khe Beach—more commonly known to Americans as China Beach. The mayor of Da Nang had originally granted the land in May 1962, and funds were donated by the many military organizations in the Da Nang area, as well as International Orphans Incorporated in California. The facility would eventually contain the Hochmuth Memorial Baby Pavilion, named in honor the late Marine Brig. Gen. Bruno Hochmuth. *National Museum of the United States Marine Corps*

A Marine "Howtar" delivers a round in response to a mortar attack. This unusual weapon married the barrel of a 4.2-inch mortar on the carriage on an M116 75 mm howitzer. Known as the M1 pack howitzer in World War II, it was so called due to its ability to be broken down and transported by pack mules. Lightweight and reliable, it continued in USMC service years after being successfully deployed in the Pacific. It was used both in this modified form and its original form during this time. The photographer has successfully captured the round as it exits the barrel. *National Museum of the United States Marine Corps*

An M107 of the Army's 2nd Battalion, 94th Artillery, receives a barrel change with the help of an M543 5-ton wrecker and an M578 LRV (light recovery vehicle). The M578 (*seen at left*) had been specifically designed to service units using the M107 SPG and M110 howitzer, and it shared the same chassis as those weapons. The location is Camp Carroll, which was located just west of Dong Ha on Route 9 and a few miles south of the DMZ. The camp had been positioned for the sole purpose of supporting operations in the DMZ area in 1966. At this time in 1968, it was home to over 2,000 men and sixty artillery pieces, including twelve M107s.

This and the following two photos depict men of the 3rd Battalion, 11th Marine Regiment, at their base at Da Nang. Members of Whiskey Battery prepare their M101A1 105 mm howitzer for action. In addition to the substantial number of sandbags present in their revetment, they have also added a raised hexagonal concrete pad. The pad is small enough to still allow the movement of the trails, as seen here. Unlike guns emplaced at remote firebases, Whiskey Battery had the resources to create positions such as this.

One of the battery's M114 155 mm guns is prepared for firing. A round is in the breech and the loader is adding a charge bag. Other crewmen stand ready with a ramrod to seat the load. The firing jack can be seen under the left wheel of the carriage. Typically, the gunner sat on the left trail in order to make adjustments to the sighting mechanism. The Marine Corps had intended that all three batteries of its divisional artillery 155 mm units be self-propelled, but both Marine divisions went to Vietnam, with only two batteries converted to the M109.

After the fire mission, the crew stands down. This shot provides a good view of the position and the surrounding area. The various buildings all have numerous sandbags added to the metal roofing material to prevent them from being blown off during a monsoon. Planks and sandbags make up the revetment, along with empty ammunition canisters. A pallet of 155 mm rounds can be seen to the rear of the gun. Like all semipermanently emplaced artillery pieces, this one is very well cared for. As was the common practice on the M114, the paint has been polished off the barrel.

Marine M76 Otters are unloaded from an LCU at the Dong Ha boat ramp. Colorful artwork adorns the lead vehicle, and the words "Cong Killer" are painted on the left side of the front hull. The boat ramp at Dong Ha sat on the Cam Lo River adjacent to the Route 1 bridge, which can be seen in the background. A portion of the concrete bridge has been replaced with several sections of Bailey bridging material.

This M48A3 Model B was photographed in the city of Hue on the morning of Friday, February 2, 1968. This is undoubtedly a tank of A Company of the 3rd Marine Tank Battalion, which was part of the small relief force sent into Hue on January 31 to relieve the embattled MACV compound on the south side of the city. The convoy was met with heavy fire as they crossed the Phu Cam Canal, as indicated by the impact marks seen here on the glass blocks beneath the commander's cupola, and the gouges on the spare track blocks. About the time this photo was taken, North Vietnamese sappers dropped the Nguyen Hoang Bridge into the Perfume River, effectively cutting the city in half.

Marines move out in the surf from their Marble Mountain base camp aboard an LVTC-5 (command version of the LVTP-5) for a sweep-and-clear operation south of Da Nang in February 1968. By this point it was common for the crews of the LVTP to create firing positions on the roof of the vehicles, using sandbags. These positions would frequently include an emplaced weapon. Although robust in automotive performance, the vehicle was quick to burn if damaged by a buried mine, forcing crews upward.

Refugees stream past an M67A2 flame tank on February 3, 1968. This tank was one of probably three flame tanks to see action in the coming battle. This photo was likely taken from one of the MACV buildings, with the gates of the Joan of Arc Church and School in the background. The church grounds would be infiltrated by NVA troops in the following days. Several sources cite the movement of civilian refuges that morning as they sought the relative safety of the MACV compound. Power lines lie on the sidewalk in the background, cut by enemy sapper teams.

This shot depicts a well-known incident involving a 106 mm Recoilless Rifle crew from 2nd Battalion, 5th Regiment, on February 3. They had disassembled and then carried a weapon into one of the classrooms of Hue University in order to fire on a machine gun team in an adjacent building. Firing the recoilless rifle via a lanyard, the scheme was effective and neutralized the enemy emplacement. The room was largely destroyed by the blast, much to the displeasure of the university staff. The crew continued using the gun in the battle after recovering it from the wreckage.

Gas mask–wearing Marines of H Company, 2nd Battalion, 5th Marines, rush a building in the Hue Post Office and Treasury complex on February 4, as the fighting moved south from the MACV compound. The platoon sergeant keeps up the pace as a radio operator stands to the left. A cache of E-8 CS gas launchers had been discovered at the MACV facility, and a quick decision was made to employ it in the house-to-house fighting that morning. The method was highly successful, since only certain NVA officers and senior NCOs carried gas masks.

LCpl. C. D. Bradford, a radioman assigned to G Company, 2nd Battalion, 5th Marines, was photographed during a smoke break on February 5, 1968. He carries a practical weapon for close-quarters fighting: a .45-caliber M1A1 Thompson submachine gun. Although not officially part of the USMC arsenal at the time, these weapons had been supplied to ARVN units, and ammunition was plentiful due to the presence of the M1911A1 pistol as well as the M3A1 grease gun used by Marine tankers. Cpl. Bradford has removed the stock for ease of movement and also carries a large bag filled with extra magazines.

Marines take cover behind vehicles in Hue on February 5. This may have been part of the small convoy from Bravo Company that had been sent to recover dead Marines in the area around the Hue Stadium. The previous night, the An Cuu Bridge over the Phu Cam Canal had been destroyed by the NVA. This severed the overland route from Phi Bai, but by this time there were already five Marine infantry companies along with tanks and supplies on the south side of the river. These units would serve as the basis for the counterattack to come.

In spite of the heavy fighting in Hue City, fighting continued in other areas for Marine Corps units. A crewman of the 3rd Tank Battalion keeps a watchful eye peeled from the cupola of his M48A3 Model B for NVA snipers in support of the 2nd Battalion, 4th Marines, east of Con Thien on February 9, 1968. This movement was a continuation of the long-running Operation Kentucky, which had begun in November 1967 to secure infiltration routes into Quang Tri Province from the DMZ. The previous day, Marine M48s had decimated a bunker complex south of Con Thien.

Marines of the 1st Battalion, 5th Marines, and an A Company M48A3 advance beside the northwest wall of the Citadel in Hue on Monday, February 12, 1968. The 1/5 was fresh to the fighting, having arrived via truck convoy from Phu Loc just the previous afternoon. Even before their arrival, the decision had been made to commit them to the Citadel. Although the ARVN had hoped to retake this historically valuable area without American help, the intense clashes of the preceding few days had ground the South Vietnamese units down past the point of combat effectiveness. The battle for the Marines would begin in earnest the next day.

A machine gun team of C Company, 1st Battalion, 5th Marine Regiment, uses a requisitioned table along with a few bricks to create an elevated firing position on Friday, February 16, 1968. C Company had spent the previous day covering the flank of D Company while they assaulted the Dong Ba gate of the Citadel. Interestingly, the Marine on the far left is using high-capacity magazines for his M16A1, seen leaning against the table. At least one other is in a pocket in his flak vest. Later that night, a radio message would be intercepted stating the NVA commander had been killed, and requesting withdrawal from the city.

Another machine gun team of C Company, 1st Battalion, 5th Regiment, hammers away at a target in the Citadel on Monday, February 19, 1968. Fighting would continue to rage there for several more days with mortar, artillery, and even limited airstrikes. A phased withdrawal of NVA forces had begun on the night of the twentieth, but the Marines fought tenaciously for every inch of the area. The destruction of the NVA command-and-supply force in the La Chu woods by the 1st Cavalry on the twenty-first hastened the final collapse on the twenty-fifth. The 1/5 would soon be shifted to the east of the city to cut off any remaining NVA forces trying to reach the coast.

An exhausted Marine Ontos crew member makes a bed of his mount on February 23, 1968. Some Marine commanders considered the Ontos to be one of the more important weapons of the urban battle, believing that if deployed properly, its mobility more than made up for its lack of heavy armor. According to after-action analysis, the 106 mm round routinely opened up to a 4-meter hole or completely knocked down interior walls at ranges of 300 to 500 meters. The weapon was still considered effective at 1,000 meters.

The heavily damaged Sick Bay at Khe Sanh Combat Base on February 24, 1968. The base had been subjected to a particularly harsh bombardment on the night of the twenty-third. This was perhaps the worst of the months-long siege—during the eight-hour barrage, over 1,300 rounds were to fall on the base. The NVA had employed Soviet-made 152 mm and 130 mm long-range artillery from bases in Laos. Ten individuals were killed in the nighttime attack, and over fifty were wounded.

Two Marines vigorously apply picks to improving the defenses of Khe Sanh on March 15, 1968. Sandbags, plywood, pallets, and gravel-filled steel drums litter the background. As the shelling intensified, the attacks were to become the focus of fervent controversy in the United States, with inevitable comparisons being made to the French siege of Dien Bien Phu. President Johnson vehemently declared that he would accept no such outcome and ordered the base to be held at all costs.

A Marine of an artillery forward observer team looks for signs of enemy movement on March 15, 1968. In late February it had been discovered that the NVA had been constructing trench lines all along the southern and southeastern portions of the perimeter. Some were within 25 meters of the wire. This trench system was intended as a jumping-off point for a future infantry attack of the base. A similar tactic had been used at Dien Bien Phu, and its discovery had a profound effect on US military planning.

A battle-scarred wall offers scant protection for men of 2nd Battalion, 4th Marines, while searching the area for NVA in Quang Tri Province during Operation Saline II, on March 12, 1968. This operation was intended to protect river traffic on the Cua Viet River. This Marine appears to be carrying a considerable amount of extra ammunition, as indicated by his bulging pockets. He also carries an entrenching tool and a rain poncho on the rear of his belt.

The busy Dong Ha boat ramp in April 1968, as Navy Rough Terrain forklifts unload cargo from Navy landing craft. The tip of a critical supply route, this facility was uniquely positioned just a few miles from the mouth of the Cua Viet River. A larger naval facility there absorbed cargo from ships off the coast for transport to Dong Ha. The boat ramp was also just a few miles from the Dong Ha Combat base, south and west of Route 1. A small hotel now occupies this property.

Marines riding atop an M48A3, christened "No Name," cover their ears as the 90 mm main gun fires during a road sweep southwest of Phu Bai on April 3, 1968. Although it was common to transport Marine infantry on board tanks, it was a hazardous practice. In Vietnam, like all wars, tanks tend to draw small-arms fire. Additionally, they were the frequent targets of mines. There are numerous incidents of multiple causalities among riding infantry as a result of mine strikes, even when the tank crews themselves were not seriously injured.

An M274 Mechanical Mule is loaded with C rations by the men of the 9th Marine Regiment at Ca Lu, near Khe Sanh, on April 22, 1968. The logistical support activity at Ca Lu was operated by Marines of the Force Logistic Command, which supplied combat units operating in that embattled area. This was officially part of Operation Scotland II, the Marine security operation that swept the area around the combat base until February of the following year.

Army crewmen load the 25,000th round into their M107 dubbed "Big Bruiser" on April 26, 1968. They are US Army members of Battery B, 8th Battalion, 4th Artillery, opcon (operational control) 11th Marines, and are firing in support of Operation Delaware. This was a substantial post-Tet joint engagement involving elements of the 1st Marine Division, the 1st Cavalry Division, the 101st Airborne Division, the 3rd Brigade of the 82nd Airborne Division, and the 196th Infantry Brigade in the A Shau valley.

This Marine command post of the 2nd Battalion, 4th Marine Regiment, was photographed on May 7, 1968, east of Dong Ha on the banks of the Cua Viet River. The communication center is a LVTC-5, the command version of the LVTP-5A1. It has been heavily bunkered with dirt and sandbags set within its forest of slender radio antennas. A power cable, probably from an auxiliary generator, runs into the hatch from the right.

Marines of the 1st Platoon, G Company, 2nd Battalion, 7th Marine Regiment, direct a concentration of fire at the enemy in a firefight on May 8, 1968. An M48A3 is seen in the background. This compelling photo was taken in the midst of Operation Allen Brook, a huge operation involving the 1st Battalion, 7th Marines; 2nd Battalion, 7th Marines; 3rd Battalion, 7th Marines; 3rd Battalion, 5th Marines; 1st Battalion, 26th Marines; 1st, 2nd, and 3rd Battalions, 27th Marines; and the 2nd Battalion, 13th Marines. Put forth to clear Go Noi Island in southern Quang Nam Province, it would account for over a thousand enemy dead.

This 1st Tank Battalion tank hit an enemy antitank mine outside a nearby hamlet while in support of D Company, 1st Battalion, 7th Marine Regiment, on May 20, 1968. The crew is beginning the unenviable task of changing the damaged section of tracks, which can just be seen in the foreground. Other photos from the sequence show that at least one road wheel was also damaged and swapped out. This photo was taken during the opening phases of Operation Mameluke Thrust, 6 miles north of An Hoa. The operation ran from May 19 through October of that year, and in addition to USMC units, it also included the 1st Squadron, 9th Cavalry.

A 4th Marine Regiment patrol enters its command post near Dong Ha after conducting an early-morning patrol along the Cua Viet River during Operation Napoleon/Saline on June 15, 1968. The Marines to the left and the right both carry M72A1 light antitank weapons. Not initially deployed in great numbers due to the lack of enemy armor, the weapons gradually gained popularity due to their effectiveness against fortified positions and bunkers. The 5-pound weapon was watertight, with its end covers closed, and the 66 mm HE warhead had a range of about 300 meters. *National Museum of the United States Marine Corps*

A Marine carries an AN/PSS-11 mine detector on his shoulder as he prepares to move out on a patrol with the 2nd Battalion, 4th Marines, along the Cua Viet River near Dong Ha on June 15, 1968. Note the headset on his helmet. He is part of Operation Napoleon, a continuation of Operation Saline II, the effort to keep the Cua Viet River supply line open. It utilized the 3rd Battalion of 1st Marines and the 1st Amphibian Tractor Battalion and had been combined on February 28. The operation would continue through the summer. *National Museum of the United States Marine Corps*

This aerial view of Hue City was taken on June 24, 1968, some four months after the conclusion of the heaviest fighting within the city. The bulk of the photograph depicts the fortresslike structures of the Citadel area, north of the Perfume River, which fills the lower third of the photo. Tran Hung Dao Street runs parallel to the river along the bottom edge of the fortress. The destroyed Nguyen Hoang Bridge can still be seen at the lower left. The Navy boat ramp is the area to the right of the destroyed bridge at the lower right.

A Marine lubricates the drive sprocket of an M76 Otter atop an elaborate structure at Camp Big John on June 29, 1968. The camp was located at Mai Xa Thi village on the Cua Viet River and had been named in honor of SMaj. John M. Malnar, who was killed in action on May 2, 1968, while fighting with the 2nd Battalion, 4th Marines. A total of five Otters operated with elements of the 1st Marine Regiment, providing medical evacuation and resupply missions to Marines conducting patrols in the area west of Cua Viet.

Two long-serving Marines, and Medal of Honor recipients, Maj. Gen. Raymond G. Davis (*right*) and Lt. Col. Archie Van Winkle, pose within the Khe Sanh combat area in July 1968. Maj. Gen. Davis, who at the time of this photo was the commanding officer of the 3rd Marine Division, was awarded his Medal of Honor for action in Korea in 1950 as a lieutenant colonel. Originally enlisting in 1938, he went on to attain the rank of full general (four stars) and retired as assistant commandant of the Marine Corps in 1971. Lt. Col. Van Winkle, who at the time of this photo was the commanding officer of the 1st Battalion, 1st Marines, was awarded his Medal of Honor for his actions as a staff sergeant in the Korean War and, like Gen. Davis, had also served in World War II, enlisting in 1942. He retired as a colonel in 1974.

A 7th Marine Regiment sniper zeroes in on a distant enemy with his Remington 700 sniper rifle, while his spotter observes, southwest of Da Nang on July 18, 1968. Also known as the Model 40, the Remington 700 was developed in 1965 by the Marine Corps Marksmanship Training Unit on the basis of the need for a bolt-action sniper rifle that would chamber the then-standard 7.62 mm NATO cartridge. Eventually, Remington's Model 40X, a version of the civilian Model 700 rifle, was chosen. Its official designation was "Rifle, 7.62 mm, Sniper, Remington M700." Later in 1969, converted M14s started entering service as the M21 sniper rifle. *National Museum of the United States Marine Corps*

This and the following photo depict a Roughrider convoy of the 7th Motor Transport Battalion from Da Nang south to the An Hoa Combat Base on July 31, 1968. Known as "Roughrider" due to their extremely hazardous nature, these convoys were under the constant threat of ambush and were always heavily armed and escorted. Here a line of M54A1 5-ton trucks proceeds along the main supply route. Originally constructed in 1966, it was then nicknamed "Liberty Road." Each of the visible trucks has a ring-mounted .50-caliber machine gun.

Elements of the convoy negotiate one of the many streams and rivers along the route thanks to a pontoon ferry and motor launch. Pauses such as this did increase the danger from ambush as vehicles waited to board. Some of the larger crossings such as that over the Thu Bon River were spanned, which was done in 1967. One of the 5-ton trucks in this shot is pulling a dolly-mounted trailer—an atypical combination. Transport of large, heavy items such as the crated ammunition seen here was practical only by road, making such convoys a military necessity regardless of the risk.

The monstrous bulk of an LVTE-1 (Landing Vehicle, Tracked, Engineer) moves toward the camera on August 15, 1968. It was supporting the 2nd Battalion, 7th Marines, in Quang Nam Province, 20 miles south of Da Nang. This was part of a larger movement known as Operation Dodge Valley that commenced on August 12 and ran until August 16. As on other Marine amphibious tractors of this time, the crew has constructed a small bunker on the top of the vehicle. The metal rack on the top hull that held the explosive line charge provided additional reinforcement. The blade shows evidence of recent use.

This sensational shot is purported to be of Operation Sussex, a clear-and-search operation held in early September 1968. However, the angle of the M101A1 howitzer indicates that the crew is dropping rounds extremely close to their own position. This photo could depict the fighting at the Thuong Duc Camp, which occurred around the same time. In this action, the NVA had launched a nearly successful attack on the camp, which was located southwest of Da Nang. The subsequent Marine response was known as Operation Maui Peak.

Korean Marines ride on top of an amphibian tractor south of Da Nang, on November 17, 1968, during a training exercise. The Koreans have mounted a 106 mm recoilless rifle on roof of this LVTP-5A1 of the 3rd Amphibian Tractor Company, 1st Marine Division. Although the Korean Marines had a reputation as fierce fighters, their American counterparts did not always see them in a good light. Friction between the units was commonplace.

Marines of the 9th Marine Regiment, 3rd Marine Division, apply a generous helping of elbow grease in order to assist an M274 Mechanical Mule over a stream in the rugged jungle-studded mountains near Laos. The 4 × 4 Mule is loaded with explosives to blow an enemy road as part of Operation Taylor Common, a multiple-battalion operation designed to disrupt enemy infiltration routes and supply operations near the Laotian border that began on December 9. All the Marines wear ERDL-pattern fatigues.

A rifleman with the 2nd Platoon L Company, 3rd Battalion, 5th Marine Regiment, returns sniper fire during Operation Meade River on November 30, 1968. This took place in the Dodge City area, which is approximately 15 miles southwest of the city of Da Nang. Also known as Operation Hung Quang, it involved nine different Marine battalions, along with the ARVN 51st Regiment. It was a cordon-and-search operation in support of the Accelerated Pacification Campaign then underway.

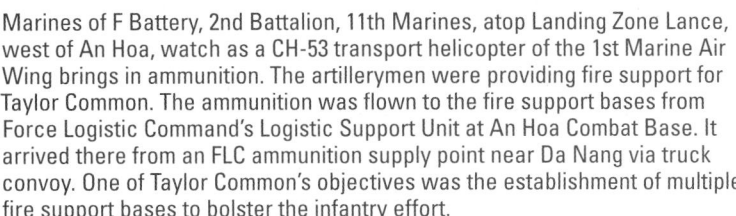

Marines of F Battery, 2nd Battalion, 11th Marines, atop Landing Zone Lance, west of An Hoa, watch as a CH-53 transport helicopter of the 1st Marine Air Wing brings in ammunition. The artillerymen were providing fire support for Taylor Common. The ammunition was flown to the fire support bases from Force Logistic Command's Logistic Support Unit at An Hoa Combat Base. It arrived there from an FLC ammunition supply point near Da Nang via truck convoy. One of Taylor Common's objectives was the establishment of multiple fire support bases to bolster the infantry effort.

A Marine CH-53 Sea Stallion helicopter places an M101A1 105 mm howitzer of the 12th Marine Regiment atop yet another Taylor Common firebase position southwest of An Hoa in mid-December. The four-month-long operation would eventually see the 1st Battalion, 3rd Marines; 3rd Battalion, 3rd Marines; 1st Battalion, 5th Marines; 2nd Battalion, 5th Marines; 3rd Battalion, 5th Marines; 2nd Battalion, 7th Marines; and 2nd and 3rd Battalions, 26th Marines all in the field.

A CH-46 comes in to drop off more equipment for the formation of one of Taylor Commons' many firebases, while an infantry company moves out on patrol. In spite of their defensive appearance with bunkers and revetments, these remote firebases were inherently offensive in nature. The emplaced artillery was meant to be a support element of aggressive patrolling, as depicted here. The amount of damage seen on this remote hilltop may indicate that this base had been formed by one of the M121 Daisy Cutter high-explosive bombs that were being experimented with at this time.

CHAPTER 4

1969–1972

Vietnamese civilians, all residents of the Batangan Peninsula, are being sheltered at the government of Vietnam's temporary relocation facility near Quang Ngai City while US Marines search for the Viet Cong on the peninsula during Operation Bold Mariner. This operation ran from January 13 through February 9 and was part of the larger Operation Game Warden. This cordon, search, and sweep operation was one of the largest amphibious assaults of the war and involved HMM-362, SLF-A, the ARVN 2nd Division, 2/26th Marines, and HMM-164.

On January 20, 1969, Richard M. Nixon was sworn in as the thirty-seventh president of the United States. He had campaigned on a platform of "Peace with Honor" in Vietnam. Beginning in July 1969, he ordered to be implemented a strategy of "Vietnamization"—the replacing of US troops with South Vietnamese troops, and phased withdrawal of US forces, including Marines, began on September 12, when the 27th Marines were returned stateside.

Operation Taylor, launched December 7, 1968, and Operation Dewey Canyon, launched February 22, 1969, both of which extended into March 1969, were primarily airmobile and firebase actions against Communist forces, both of which destroyed vast amounts of enemy materiel. Dewey Canyon was the Marines' first major incursion into Laos.

On June 7, 1969, a PAVN sapper tossed a satchel charge into a bunker at An Hoa Combat Base, killing four Marines, one of whom was PFC Dan Bullock. Bullock had forged his age to join the Marine Corps, and though claiming to be twenty was in fact only fifteen years old, thus becoming the youngest Marine to die in the war.

The redeployment of Marines from Vietnam, now code-named "Keystone Robin," accelerated in early 1970, with the 26th Marines and MAG-12 returning home. In October of the year, the 7th Marines began leaving Vietnam, and the 5th Marines followed in March 1971.

In April 1971, the III MAF Headquarters, along with the headquarters of the 1st Marine Division and 1st MAW, all left Vietnam. The next month the Marine civic action and pacification campaign ended when the Combined Action Group Headquarters were deactivated. In June, the 3rd Marine Amphibious Brigade was deactivated, bringing to a close major Marine Corps operations in Vietnam.

In April 1972, MAG-15 was deployed to Da Nang, and the next month MAG-12 was deployed to Bien Hoa, both under the command of the 7th Air Force in support of the South Vietnamese air force. MAG-15 redeployed to Thailand in June. While ground forces were embarked and in the Gulf of Tonkin, they did not land. The last Marine tactical unit left Vietnam on March 14, 1973, and on August 14, 1973, combat air operations over Vietnam by the Marines ceased.

Escorted by Maj. Gen. Raymond G. Davis (*right*), commanding general of the 3rd Marine Division, Lt. Gen. Henry W. Buse Jr. (*center*), commanding general of the Fleet Marine Force Pacific, visits Marine units located at Cam Lo on January 25, 1969. Gen. Buse was visiting Vietnam on his regular inspection tour. Maj. Gen. Davis is wearing the Coat, Man's Combat Tropical, Camouflage, Lightweight, with its matching trousers, both in ERDL pattern. These items would become more common in USMC units throughout 1969.

Marine UH-1E helicopters touch down with their loads at Fire Support Base Cunningham on January 26, 1969. They were supporting elements of the 9th Marines conducting search-and-clear operations during Operation Dewey Canyon. This offensive was specifically directed against NVA communication lines in Laos north of the A Shau valley. Participating units were the 1st Battalion, 9th Marines; 2nd Battalion, 9th Marines; 3rd Battalion, 9th Marines; 2nd Battalion, 3rd Marines; and the ARVN 2nd Regiment

On the morning of February 3, 1969, Maj. Gen. Ormand Simpson, commanding general of 1st Marine Division, introduces members of the Task Force Yankee Staff to South Vietnamese president Nguyen Van Thieu. President Thieu stops to talk to Maj. R. E. Simmons, commanding officer of 1st Force Recon. Army Maj. William E. Moulton Jr., senior advisor to the 1st ARVN Ranger Battalion, is at the far right.

A Soviet-manufactured ATS-59 tracked prime mover stands immobilized in the jungle of the A Shau valley complex on February 24, 1969. This fully tracked artillery tractor had been used by the North Vietnamese army to move supplies, where it was no doubt highly valued for use along the rugged jungle trails. Marine infantrymen of the 9th Marine Regiment captured it during Operation Dewey Canyon.

Marine-towed 155 mm guns perched on top of Fire Support Base Cutlass point out over the operational area of Operation Taylor Common in February 1969. This is just one of several firebases that were set up to assist during the massive operation held from December 1968 through March 1969. The purpose of these bases was to interdict NVA infiltration routes from the Laotian border, as well as assist ground troops in clearing the An Hoa basin. This area was also home to the notorious NVA Base Area 11, which was to be neutralized by these efforts. *National Museum of the United States Marine Corps*

Marines check out their brand-new M107 175 mm self-propelled guns located at Camp Muir on Hill 55. The USMC had just converted their independent artillery batteries to the M107 at this time, finally retiring their venerable, but aging, fleet of M53 and M55 self-propelled guns—at the time of their retirement, the USMC was their sole remaining user. Bearing some resemblance to its World War II cousin, the 155 mm "Long Tom," the M107 was a considerable technological leap ahead. In Vietnam its extreme long range made it deadly in engaging targets—it could hurl a 147-pound projectile some 21 miles.

This shot depicts the firing of the first M107s at Hill 55 in support of the 7th Marine Regiment, 1st Marine Division, on March 5, 1969. A battery from the 11th Marine Artillery Regiment mans the guns. Hill 55 is also known as Camp Muir, named after Lt. Col. Joseph Muir, CO of the 3rd Battalion, 3rd Marines, who was killed on September 11, 1965. A base had been established there in late early February 1966, and it was located about 10 miles southwest of Da Nang.

Marines of G Battery, 3rd Battalion, 11th Marine Regiment, prepare to fire an M101A1 105 mm howitzer in support of the 7th Marine Regiment during Operation Oklahoma Hills. They are firing from Hill 63, 25 miles southwest of the city of Da Nang. Metal slat material has been laid at the bottom of the revetment to provide a smooth surface for the gun. Fairly elaborate ammunition storage lockers have been fabricated from empty wooden ammunition crates (probably filled with sand), further secured with sandbags and plywood.

Marines of the 7th Marine Regiment disembark from a CH-53 atop Hill 502, west-southwest of Da Nang, during Operation Oklahoma Hills. This multiple-battalion operation was directed at NVA units in and around Happy Valley and was conducted alongside the ARVN 51st Regiment from March 31 to May 29, 1969. The Marines are all heavily laden with gear for what will be an extended combat patrol. The individual at the far left carries a 5-gallon water container to top off the many canteens of his platoon before they begin their march. *National Museum of the United States Marine Corps*

Marines fire an M101A1 105 mm howitzer at enemy positions from Fire Support Base Ross, 26 miles south of Da Nang, Vietnam. The men are assigned to the 3rd Battalion, 11th Marine Regiment, which fires in support of the 2nd Battalion, 7th Marine Regiment, during Oklahoma Hills. A substantial stack of rounds sits beneath the breech, indicating a sustained fire mission. The waist-high breech made loading a relatively simple task, and a good crew was capable of throwing ten rounds down range per minute, although three was more practical in most cases. *National Museum of the United States Marine Corps*

An LVTH-6 fires in support of ground troops on Operation Oklahoma Hills on April 6, 1969. As befitting its adopted role as a land-bound SPG, the vehicle sits within a sandbagged position. A structure or tarp has been added over the forward ramp to increase the interior space. A folding chair adorns the mantlet. The 105 mm weapon of the LVTH-6 would have been highly useful in the bunker-busting role; however, the vulnerability of the chassis to RPG and mine damage made it unsuitable for direct combat.

Two tanks from C Company, 1st Tank Battalion, 3rd Platoon, stop and look over the terrain situation before moving on during Operation Pipestone Canyon, 8 miles south of Da Nang, on June 2, 1969. The operation was another attempt to retake the Go Noi Island area, and it involved four USMC units as well as the ROK 2nd Marine Brigade. The massive sweep was conducted for months—from May 26 through November 7. This photo was likely taken just prior to C Company's assault on enemy bunkers on the afternoon of June 2.

Marine mortar men with the 5th Marine Regiment prepare mortar rounds for firing during the opening phases of Operation Pipestone Canyon. Fused and ready to go, the rounds are stored near the mortar tubes for instant response to calls for fire on enemy positions. Although not visible in the shot, their weapon is the long-serving M2 60 mm mortar. The M2 had been in service with US forces for nearly thirty years at this point. The rounds being readied are the M49A2 high-explosive type. *National Museum of the United States Marine Corps*

Company D of the 1st Battalion, 7th Marines, starts climbing aboard their amphibious tractors on the way into Arizona Territory on July 2, 1969, during Operation Forsythe Grove. Held from June 30 through July 3, participating units also included the 1st Battalion and the 2nd Battalion, 5th Marines. This photo provides a good perspective of the sheer size of the LVTP-5A1—it stood nearly 3 meters, or 9.6 feet. Several of the Marines in this shot still carry their M14 rifles.

This dramatic shot depicts a CH-46 pulling away after inserting the entirety of G Company, 2nd Battalion, 4th Marines, at Fire Support Base Pete in the Mutters Ridge area on September 20, 1969. Mutter's Ridge was the name given by Marines to the Nui Cay Tre (also known as Bamboo Mountain) ridge, in Quang Tri Province. The ridge was formed by Hills 461, 484, and 400 and overlooked the southern edge of the Demilitarized Zone to the north and Route 9 to the south.

The USMC began their withdrawal from the Vandegrift Combat Base at the end of September 1969. Here, bulldozers of the 71st Engineers Headquarters level and regrade the food storage area on September 26. The base had been established as Landing Zone Stud in early 1968 by the 1st Cavalry Division to support the relief of Khe Sanh. It was located off Route 9 north of Ca Lu and east of Khe Sanh. Named after the former Marine Corps commandant and Medal of Honor winner, the base had served as support for Operation Dewey Canyon. Turned over to the ARVN 2nd Division, it was dismantled and used to reinforce Camp Carroll.

Marines of the 3rd Platoon, I Company, 3rd Battalion, 1st Marine Regiment, on a reconnaissance patrol 8 miles south of Da Nang on October 30, 1969. The Marine in the middle is carrying either a PRC-25 or PRC-77 radio set. Both transistorized radios were nearly identical and were designed as replacements for the awful AN/PRC-10 tubed radios that had so plagued small-unit communications in the early stages of the conflict. The Marines began adopting the new radios in 1967.

This picturesque shot depicts fishermen returning to their old fishing grounds on the two rivers surrounding Go Noi Island after moving into the village of Phu Loc. The village is part of the government of the Republic of Vietnam's resettlement and is located 14 miles south of Da Nang. This area had been the scene of fierce fighting for years, and much of the land on the island had been defoliated by Rome plows in order to deny cover to Viet Cong units. *National Museum of the United States Marine Corps*

High atop Dong Ha Mountain, at Fire Support Base Fuller, Marines ready their M101A1 105 mm howitzer for a fire mission. They are attached to A Battery, 1st Battalion, 12th Marine Regiment. Fire Support Base Fuller was the northernmost firebase in Vietnam. Overlooking the DMZ, Dong Ha Mountain stood 1,800 feet high, and the base was only 35 yards at the widest spot. The regiment's crest, indicating the battery and the battalion, can be seen on the right side of the gun shield. *National Museum of the United States Marine Corps*

A member of Company A, 1st Battalion, 7th Marines, 1st Marine Division, samples some sugar cane during a harvest break near Monge Hong village, 21 miles southeast of Da Nang. The unit had helped provide security for the harvest. An M116A1 Husky passes by in the background. The Husky was the replacement for the Marine Corps' aging fleet of M76 Otters. Blaw-Knox Company built the M116 for the US Army, while Pacific Car & Foundry built the similar M116A1 for the Navy and Marine Corps. *National Museum of the United States Marine Corps*

Boats bring produce and fish to the Dong Ha Market in Hue City. This type of river-borne commence had been the basis for the Vietnamese economy for centuries. Looming over the market, heavily damaged during Tet, is the new market building. Construction of the building, halted during the offensive of the previous year, is proceeding at a rapid pace at the date of this photo in the summer of 1969. *National Museum of the United States Marine Corps*

PFC Brad Glaser, a mortarman with 1st Battalion, 5th Marine Regiment, carries a 60 mm mortar tube on his shoulder as he moves out on a sweep in the Arizona Territory, 17 miles southwest of Da Nang, Vietnam. Pvt. Glaser wears his M55 flak vest over his OD T-shirt, a practical combination in the heat. He has placed local foliage in the slits of his helmet cover. Although designed for just this purpose, it wasn't often done. *National Museum of the United States Marine Corps*

This sensational shot shows Marines of the 2nd Battalion, 4th Marine Regiment, firing their 81 mm mortar during night engagement just south of the Demilitarized Zone in Quang Tri Province. The M29 81 mm mortar was the standard heavy mortar of the USMC at this time, having replaced the World War II M1 mortar during the Korean conflict. Easily broken down, it could be carried by a three-man team. Five men typically crewed the weapon, which could fire to a maximum range of about 4,000 yards.

Ready to be loaded for its 20-mile trip, a 150-pound projectile is readied for loading by Marines of the 1st 175 mm Gun Battery (SP). The 175 mm gun batteries, like the 155 mm batteries before them, were independent batteries and were capable of performing their own administrative functions similar to that of a battalion. At this time, four of the five Marine Corps artillery batteries saw action in Vietnam: the 1st, 3rd, 5th, and 7th. The remaining battery (the 2nd) was assigned to the 2nd Field Artillery Group and was based at Camp Lejeune in North Carolina. The 1st Battery was placed under the operational control of the 11th Artillery Regiment.

Stateside bound: five completely rebuilt M76 Otters sit in a row at Force Logistic Command's Motor Transport Maintenance Company in the fall of 1969. The Marines there had worked for three weeks to reconstruct the amphibious vehicles so that they could travel back the United States for use in training. After over a decade of use, they were to be replaced in USMC service by the M116A1 Husky.

CH-46 helicopters of Marine Helicopter Squadron Medium 165 (HMM-165) prepare to depart for a combat mission. They are arranged on a large stand that had been constructed from earth and would allow additional clearance from the rotor blades for the troops entering the helicopters. The large winglets on either side of the CH-46 had no lift capabilities and served only to act as aerodynamic enclosures for the landing gear.

A gunner with B Company, 1st Tank Battalion, cleans and oils his .50-caliber machine gun on its sky mount mounted atop the tank's empty .50-caliber turret. At the time of this photo, the unit was based at Hill 55, a hilltop combat base 8 miles southwest of Da Nang, and was supporting the 1st Marine Regiment. Indicative of the fierce fighting that was often characteristic of infantry supporting armor operations, the crew has added caricature kill markings to the right side of the turret. The proliferation of rocket-propelled grenades meant that every enemy infantryman was a potential threat.

A fire team leader with the 3rd Platoon of L Company, 3rd Battalion, 1st Marines, observes his perimeter while on an extended patrol 8 miles south of the city of Da Nang. He has created a temporary fighting position by digging a foxhole behind a line of small trees. An extra bandolier of 5.56 mm ammunition magazines hangs on a branch in front of him for easy access. Although the ERDL-pattern fatigue had a drawstring at the bottom of each leg, this Marine has elected to roll them up to keep them from getting wet. *National Museum of the United States Marine Corps*

A Marine prepares to drop a round into an M2 60 mm mortar on January 14, 1970. He and his team are engaged in the area of Hill 190, 4 miles northwest of Da Nang. One of the advantages of the M2 was that it could be set up and used quite quickly—a situation that is certainly being played out here. Although the prone Marine is providing stability by gripping the tripod, both men would no doubt seek another position for extended fire of the weapon. *National Museum of the United States Marine Corps*

Vietnamese villagers from Monge Hong, 21 miles south of Da Nang, use a traditional woven structure to harvest their rice crop on April 15, 1970. Members of Company A, 1st Battalion, 7th Marines, 1st Marine Division, joined forces with Vietnamese Popular Force soldiers to provide security for the harvest. *National Museum of the United States Marine Corps*

On July 15, 1970, Company B of 2nd Battalion of the 7th Marines exit their landing CH-46 helicopters to join in on Operation Pickens Forest. This operation was conducted by the 1st and 2nd Battalions of the 7th Marines and was a typical clear-and-search operation held near Song Thu Bon valley, Quang Nam Province, from July 15 through August 24. All the visible Marines wear their ripstop ERDL-pattern fatigue trousers and carry extra gear and ammunition for an extended march.

Plane captains of Marine Attack Squadron (VMA) 311 mix laundry soap with water to wash grime and dirt from their A-4E Skyhawks. The washing is necessary to prevent corrosion and clogging of moving parts on the exterior of the plane. Lpl. William E. Lysle (Burbank, California), *left*, and LCpl. Porter R. Tkachuk (Boston, Massachsetts). VMA-311 operated from Chu Lai from May 1965, until relocating to Da Nang in the summer of 1970. By the time the unit withdrew on January 29, 1973, having flown 54,625 combat sorties flown and dropped 105,000 tons of ordnance.

"The Brass" photographed on July 8, 1970, during a tour of 7th Marines at Fire Support Base Ryder, 27 miles south-southwest of Da Nang. Left to right are Col. E. G. Derning Jr., commanding officer of 7th Marines; Lt. Gen. J. W. Sutherland, commander of the Army's XXIV Corps; and Maj. Gen. Charles F. Widdecke, commanding general of 1st Marine Division. Maj. Gen. Widdecke was a decorated veteran of the Pacific campaign, having received a Silver Star for action on Eniwetok Atoll and a Navy Cross for action on Guam in 1944. He assumed command in April 1970 after Maj. Gen. Edwin B. Wheeler was injured in a helicopter crash.

An M101A1 105 mm howitzer firing from Fire Support Base Defiant on July 20, 1970, in support of Operation Pickens Forest. The photographer has captured the gun in full recoil, as the loader stands by with another round. The M1 high-explosive round of the M101A1 weighed around 43 pounds, making ammunition handling relatively easy for healthy young men. All the crewmen wear their ERDL-pattern fatigue trousers and M55 flak vests, although the Marine second from the right has acquired a newer M69 flak vest.

Marines from Company, 3rd Battalion, 26th Marines, who have been brought into Elephant Valley by CH-46 helicopters move out of the landing zone in one of the battalion's last operations. The battalion was scheduled to redeploy with the 26th Marines for Operation Keystone Robin. This operation utilized the Marine units as covering force for the redeployment of the 3rd Brigade of the 9th Infantry Division and the 199th Infantry Brigade from Vietnam to the United States in October 1970.

Due to its relatively light weight, the M101A1 howitzer could be rapidly airlifted into remote areas to provide immediate fire support. This was often the case with the many firebases found throughout Vietnam during the US military's involvement there. Although those applications were typically on high ground, these methods could be employed in any location. This unit is conducting a fire demonstration after just such a deployment during an exercise for ARVN units known as Escort Lion II, in December 1970. *National Museum of the United States Marine Corps*

With the introduction of the AH-1G Cobra into Army service in 1967, the USMC requested seventy-two of the new helicopters for each of the attack squadrons in the three Marine air wings. However, permission was received to incorporate only thirty-eight helicopters, the first of which went into action in April 1969. This AH-1G is being put through its paces at the Marble Mountain Air Facility. Tragically, two AH-1Gs and their crews were lost in April due to a midair collision. A Marine-specific version, the AH-1J Sea Cobra, eventually went into production and was evaluated in Vietnam in 1971.

This Vietnamese farmer gives a skeptical look while watching a Force Logistic Command–sponsored farm machinery demonstration in Da Son, near Da Nang, in late 1970. Known officially as the 1st Force Service Regiment, Force Logistic Command, Fleet Marine Force, this unit was responsible for all manner of logistical activities related to the USMC's deployment in Vietnam. Like the rest of the Marine Corps, they participated heavily in pacification efforts and often showcased modern Western farming equipment. This was seen as a way to lessen the burden on the poor rural Vietnamese farmers. *National Museum of the United States Marine Corps*

Marine grenadier PFC Michael C. Trinwith discusses searching procedures with a South Vietnamese Ranger, MSgt. Ngo Si Hung, during a recent sweep of villages north of FLC perimeter by the Provisional Rifle Company. This shot provides a good view of the M79 grenade launcher and its large sight. Pvt. Trinwith still wears his M55 flak vest, whether by design or necessity. The later M69 series of vests is decidedly scarce in period USMC photos.

Members of Battery W, 3rd Battalion, 11th Marines, adjust the site on their 4.2-inch mortar tube. Whiskey Battery was stationed at Landing Zone Baldy. The M30 4.2-inch mortar was a heavy-rifled mortar that could hurl a 26-pound high-explosive round 6,500 yards downrange. Because of its 626-pound weight, it was typically used within fixed positions. LZ Baldy and Hill 63 composed a fire support base located Northwest of Chu Lai, Quang Nam Province, about 20 miles southwest of Da Nang, and was jointly held by Army logistics units.

Marines of Company E, 2nd Battalion, 5th Marines, negotiate rocky terrain as they search the ridgelines in the Que Son Mountains on January 25, 1971. This area was located about 23 miles southwest of Da Nang and was always heavily contested. The lead Marine is outfitted simply for a combat patrol, wearing his M55 flak vest over an OG 109 T-shirt, atop his ERDL ripstop trousers. An ammunition bandolier sits across his chest, and he carries one additional can of 7.62 mm belts, essential to feed his unit's M60 machine gun.

A Marine makes a final check on the alignment of his M101A1 105 mm howitzer before it is fired during a fire mission from Fire Support Base Rider on February 10, 1971. This well-used firing position has been equipped with wooden planks over a sandbag base, although long use appears to have compressed it significantly. Empty fiberboard containers have been stacked around the gun in order to create the walls of the revetment. A wooden ammunition crate sits in the foreground, ready to be opened.

Cpl. Ural Hunter and his sentry dog Fritz take the point position as his Combined Action Platoon begins another day of patrolling near Vieh Hao. The CAP initiative is considered to be one of the most successful counterinsurgency tools developed during the Vietnam War. Created by Marine Maj. Gen. Lewis Walt in 1965, the basic concept was to combine a thirteen-man Marine rifle squad with local forces to form village defense platoons. The program was highly successful in denying the enemy sanctuary at the local level. Cpl. Hunter has acquired an M69 flak vest. This is an earlier version with the zipper. *National Museum of the United States Marine Corps*

A Marine CH-53 Sea Stallion helicopter from a Marine heavy helicopter squadron hovers over the pickup zone prior to lifting a load of ammunition from an MR-1 combat base on February 12, 1971. The ammunition was delivered to ARVN forces engaged in Operation Lam Son 719 inside Laos. The operation ran from February 9 through March 25. The Army Rough Terrain forklift in the foreground has its ROPS device in place, unlike so many previous pictured Marine forklifts. *National Museum of the United States Marine Corps*

A large convoy of M52 semitrailers and M54 5-ton trucks manned by members of the 3rd Battalion, 5th Marines, prepare to leave for the last time from Combat Base Ross on February 14, 1971, prior to returning to the United States. They will travel by truck to Hill 34 and turn over the firebase to the South Vietnamese. Sandbags have been placed on the roofs of many of the base's buildings to prevent the material from blowing away during the typhoon season. The fortresslike nature of Combat Base Ross is apparent here in the large lookout towers and the extensive barbed-wire fixtures.

An M51 tank retriever assists an M109 of the 11th Marines near the Combat Base Baldy airstrip on March 5, 1971. The M51 was based on the chassis of the M103 heavy tank. Although no M103s were sent to Vietnam, the M51 was a still a vital component of the Marine armor contingent. Gasoline powered, the massive vehicle was capable of pulling two M48s, and the M109 presented no problems. The mast of a California state flag has been inserted into the gear rack on the left side of the turret, and the words "California or bust" have been scrawled on the lower hull. The convoy was moving from Combat Base Ross, 26 miles southeast of Da Nang, for eventual redeployment to Camp Pendleton. *National Museum of the United States Marine Corps*

Although engaged for many years in ground operations in Vietnam, the USMC was still, at its heart, an amphibious force. Aptly demonstrating this fact is this Marine M109 being loaded on USS *Pitkin County* (LST-1082) as it prepares to depart for the United States on March 3, 1971. The USS *Pitkin County* was built in 1945 as the LST-1082 and served in the Okinawan campaign, as well as the occupation of Japan and the Korean conflict. Given a name in addition to a number in 1955, she was also decommissioned that year and placed in the Reserve Fleet. Recommissioned in 1966, she served until 1971, when she was decommissioned for the final time.

F-4B Phantom IIs of Marine Fighter Attack Squadron (VMFA) 115, are in flight over South Vietnam, carrying ordnance supplies. VMFA-115, the "Able Eagles," were deployed at Da Nang Air Base from October 14, 1965, until March 1971, flying their last combat mission in Vietnam on February 22, 1971. During their deployment, the unit flew over 34,000 combat sorties.

An M101A1 105 mm howitzer team prepares for a fire mission on March 11, 1971. The photograph was taken at Fire Support Base Ryder, 27 miles southwest of Da Nang in the Que Son Mountains. The men are serving with the 2nd Battalion, 11th Marines. In the background, tarps cover their ammunition storage area, and at least one can be seen marked "HE," for high explosive. Proper organization of their ammunition supply would mean better response time during fire missions. *National Museum of the United States Marine Corps*

Marines from a battery of Headquarters Regiment, 11th Marines, 1st Marine Division, give their 4.2-inch mortar a workout on a fire mission from a position in the Que Son Mountains, 19 miles south of Da Nang, on March 5, 1971. This slightly raised shot provides a good prospective of the massive weapon and its substantial round. Prolonged use has caused the heavy baseplate to sink into the earth. Because of its large size, the Army created a self-propelled version based on the M113 chassis, known as the M106. *National Museum of the United States Marine Corps*

A mechanic from Company C, 11th Motor Transport Battalion, 1st Marine Division, checks out the mechanism beneath the fifth wheel of an M52 tractor on March 11, 1971. The M52 was a derivative of the well-known M54 5-ton truck and was used extensively in Vietnam. It is one of the forty-one trucks used to haul food, ammunition, and heavy equipment to the Khe Sanh Combat Base. The long drive succeeded in assisting the US Army in supplying the ARVN, who were then involved in destroying the vital arteries of the Ho Chi Minh Trail in Laos. *National Museum of the United States Marine Corps*

A Marine forklifts two crates of rice destined for the ARVN drive into Laos from Khe Sanh Combat Base on March 11, 1971. Behind him is Hill 950, which was defended successfully by the Marines during the 1968 siege. Although the base had been largely abandoned in July 1968, it had been reactivated to support Operation Lam Son 719 in February. It would be abandoned again in early April. *National Museum of the United States Marine Corps*

Marines serving with the 1st Reconnaissance Battalion, 1st Marine Division, patiently await their insertion from a CH-46 helicopter into the rugged Que Son Mountains, 21 miles south of Da Nang. The Marines are participating in a search-and-clear operation, Operation Imperial Lake, which was conducted from August 31, 1970, to May 12, 1971. Units deployed were the 1st Battalion, 5th Marines; 2nd Battalion, 5th Marines; and the 3rd Battalion, 5th Marines. *National Museum of the United States Marine Corps*

Elements of the 1st Battalion, 5th Marine Regiment, prepare for a lift from Hill 510 in the Que Son Mountains to Hill 34 near Da Nang to begin stand-down procedures on March 24, 1971. Hill 510 was the last combat outpost for the battalion prior to redeployment from Vietnam. A large helipad has been marked out on the hilltop, using sandbags. In addition to their ERDL-pattern uniforms, several of the Marines carry the Tropical Rucksack with its associated tubular frame.

Three artillerymen of the 1st Battalion, 11th Marine Regiment, 1st Marine Division, prepare their M101A1 105 mm howitzer for a firing mission in the Que Son Mountains, 21 miles south of Da Nang, on April 13, 1971. The Marine in the foreground cleans the breech mechanism while the other two clean and lubricate the weapon. The breechblock has been removed from the weapon and is sitting at his feet. *National Museum of the United States Marine Corps*

Two LCMs from USS *Denver* (LPD-9) transport 1st Platoon, C Company, 3rd Tank Battalion, 9th Marines, toward transports on June 14, 1972. The unit had boarded their LCMs at Hue City and moved down the coast toward Da Nang, where they were loaded on ships bound for Okinawa. Both tanks are Model B variants of the M48A3, and both have their turrets trained rearward with their 90 mm guns locked for travel. Both also have their snorkels in place—standard procedure on any amphibious operation.

On April 12, 1975, the Marines began Operation Eagle Pull, evacuating American and other foreign nationals from Phnom Penh, Cambodia, just before the fall of the city to the Communist Cambodian Khmer Rouge. This was a precursor for a similar action.

Following the breaking of the peace accords, and with the fall of South Vietnam inevitable, on April 29, 1975, the Marines launched Operation Frequent Wind, the rapid evacuation of Americans, foreign nationals, and various Vietnamese officials and citizens endangered due to their association with Americans from Saigon to ships of the US 7th Fleet. On this day, twenty-one-year-old Cpl. Charles McMahon and nineteen-year-old LCpl. Darwin Judge, members of the Marine Security Guard, were killed in a rocket attack on the Defense Attaché Office, Saigon, becoming the last Marines to die in the country of Vietnam. The next day, the last man to leave the embassy was MSgt. Juan Valdez, commander of the Marine Security Guard at the Saigon embassy, who brought with him the American flag.

This should have been the final Marine operation of the Vietnam War, but the next month the Marines answered the call to arms once more.

On May 12, the Khmer Rouge captured the civilian container ship SS *Mayaguez* in international waters in the Gulf of Thailand, along with its crew. Two days later, eight helicopters attempted to land 600 BLT 2/9 Marines on Koh Tang Island, where the crew was believed to be held, and Marines from Company D, 1st Battalion, 4th Marines, boarded the *Mayaguez*. The ship was deserted. These operations resulted in eighteen Americans being killed, with a further twenty-three USAF security policemen from the 56th Security Police Force dying in a related helicopter crash. Ultimately, the Khmer Rouge released the *Mayaguez* crew, who were picked up by the destroyer USS *Henry B. Wilson* at sea.

Following the withdrawal under fire from Koh Tang, it was discovered that LCpl. Joseph N. Hargrove, PFC Gary L. Hall, and Pvt. Danny G. Marshall had been inadvertently left behind. The Marines ashore radioed the Marines at sea, asking when the next helicopter was coming. Unfortunately, RAdm. Robert P. Coogan, under 7th Fleet orders to cease hostile actions, and believing that a rescue attempt would be met with gunfire that he could not return, refused to mount a rescue. The three men were subsequently captured and, tragically, executed, becoming the final Marines to give their all in the war.

USMC Casualties in Vietnam	
11,490	Killed in action
1,481	Died of wounds
109	Missing in action, presumed dead
9	Prisoner of war, died in captivity
13,089	Total fatalities
51,392	Wounded in action
64,481	TOTAL COMBAT CASUALTIES

Marines of the 2nd Battalion Landing Team, 4th Marine Regiment, head across the flight deck of the USS *Okinawa* to board helicopters during Operation Eagle Pull on the morning of April 12, 1975. This operation was conducted in order to evacuate US citizens, at-risk Cambodians, and third-country nationals from the Cambodian capital, Phnom Penh, prior to its imminent capture by the Khmer Rouge. The Marines will provide ground security for the operation after being transported by CH-53Ds of HMH-462. *National Museum of the United States Marine Corps*

Marines of H Company, 2nd Battalion Landing Team, 4th Marine Regiment, charge out of a CH-53D on the flight deck of the USS *Okinawa* after returning from Landing Zone Hotel in Phnom Penh during Operation Eagle Pull. The evacuation landing zone was a soccer field located northeast of the US embassy and was selected due to its distance from the direct-fire weapons of the Khmer Rouge. Other than their M16A1 rifles, there is little to distinguish these Marines from those of the initial landing force that went ashore ten years earlier.

Marines from Company D, 1st Battalion, 4th Marines, stand on board the merchant ship SS *Mayaguez* following its recovery on May 14, 1975, near Koh Tang Island, Cambodia. An escort ship, USS *Harold E. Holt* (DE-1074), had come alongside the *Mayaguez*, and the Marines had stormed it using tear gas to prevent physical injury to the crewmen. No one was aboard, and the *Mayaguez* crewmen were later returned. Although the Marines pictured here still wear their solid-color cotton fatigues, they all sport new ERDL-pattern helmet covers.

Although the original caption states otherwise, it is likely that this photo depicts a CH-53, call sign "Knive 22," after it crash-landed in Trat Province on the coast of Thailand. It had sustained heavy damage during the initial assault of Koh Tang Island on May 15, 1975. After successfully providing covering fire for other helicopters in the assault force, it was damaged so severely that the CH-53 and its passengers were escorted to the Thai coast by two other aircraft. All service members were eventually returned to the Royal Thai naval base at U-Tapao. *National Museum of the United States Marine Corps*